Regimes of Value in Tourism

Drawing from ethnographic work in five continents, this book demonstrates how different regimes of value in tourism can coexist, collide, and compete across a varied geographic terrain. Much theory in tourism economics defines 'value' as a measure of monetary worth, a concept governing commodity exchange, and a gauge for tourist satisfaction. The research included in this volume shows that tourism not only feeds off existing conceptions of value as a monetary category, but that it is also instrumental in reproducing and reinforcing those subjective, morally heightened, and highly intangible values that make tourism and the tourism economy a complex social, cultural, political, and psychological phenomenon. The book pushes the debate about the tourism economy beyond a simplistic understanding of producer-consumer relations, instead suggesting a refocus on the social, spatial, and temporal lags in tourism production, and the ensuing differentiated regimes of values.

This book was published as a special issue of the *Journal of Tourism and Cultural Change*.

Émilie Crossley is a critical psychologist whose work explores tourist subjectivity from the perspective of psychosocial studies. She holds a PhD from Cardiff University, UK, and currently works at Otago Polytechnic in New Zealand. Her research interests include volunteer tourism, tourists' perceptions of poverty, spatialities of care, and longitudinal methods.

David Picard is an anthropologist working at the University of Lusanne, Switzerland, with research interests in tourism and travel culture, hospitality, nature conservation, science and epistemology, and winemaking. He has led research projects in the Indian Ocean, Australia, Portugal, South America, and Antarctica.

Regimes of Value in Tourism

Edited by
Émilie Crossley and David Picard

LONDON AND NEW YORK

First published 2016
by Routledge
2 Park Square, Milton Park, Abingdon, Oxon, OX14 4RN, UK

and by Routledge
711 Third Avenue, New York, NY 10017, USA

First issued in paperback 2017

Routledge is an imprint of the Taylor & Francis Group, an informa business

British Library Cataloguing in Publication Data
A catalogue record for this book is available from the British Library

ISBN 13: 978-1-138-10679-6 (pbk)
ISBN 13: 978-1-138-93637-9 (hbk)

Typeset in Times
by RefineCatch Limited, Bungay, Suffolk

Publisher's Note
The publisher accepts responsibility for any inconsistencies that may have
arisen during the conversion of this book from journal articles to book chapters,
namely the possible inclusion of journal terminology.

Disclaimer
Every effort has been made to contact copyright holders for their permission to
reprint material in this book. The publishers would be grateful to hear from any
copyright holder who is not here acknowledged and will undertake to rectify
any errors or omissions in future editions of this book.

Contents

Citation Information

The chapters in this book were originally published in the *Journal of Tourism and Cultural Change*, volume 12, issue 3 (September 2014). When citing this material, please use the original page numbering for each article, as follows:

Chapter 1
Editorial: Regimes of value in tourism
Émilie Crossley and David Picard
Journal of Tourism and Cultural Change, volume 12, issue 3 (September 2014)
pp. 201–205

Chapter 2
Tourism as theatre: performing and consuming indigeneity in an Australian wildlife sanctuary
David Picard, Celmara Pocock and David Trigger
Journal of Tourism and Cultural Change, volume 12, issue 3 (September 2014)
pp. 206–223

Chapter 3
Shifting values of 'primitiveness' among the Zafimaniry of Madagascar: an anthropological approach to tourist mediators' discourses
Fabiola Mancinelli
Journal of Tourism and Cultural Change, volume 12, issue 3 (September 2014)
pp. 224–236

Chapter 4
Branding Copán: valuing cultural distinction in an archaeological tourism destination
Lena Mortensen
Journal of Tourism and Cultural Change, volume 12, issue 3 (September 2014)
pp. 237–252

Chapter 5
Values of property (properties of value): capitalization of kinship in Norway
Simone Abram
Journal of Tourism and Cultural Change, volume 12, issue 3 (September 2014)
pp. 253–266

Chapter 6

Value of silence: mediating aural environments in Estonian rural tourism
Maarja Kaaristo
Journal of Tourism and Cultural Change, volume 12, issue 3 (September 2014)
pp. 267–279

Chapter 7

From tourist to person: the value of intimacy in touristic Cuba
Valerio Simoni
Journal of Tourism and Cultural Change, volume 12, issue 3 (September 2014)
pp. 280–292

For any permission-related enquiries please visit:
http://www.tandfonline.com/page/help/permissions

Notes on Contributors

Simone Abram is based in the International Centre for Research in Events, Tourism and Hospitality at Leeds Beckett University, Leeds, UK, and in the Department of Anthropology at Durham University, UK.

Émilie Crossley is a critical psychologist whose work explores tourist subjectivity from the perspective of psychosocial studies. She holds a PhD from Cardiff University, UK, and currently works at Otago Polytechnic in New Zealand. Her research interests include volunteer tourism, tourists' perceptions of poverty, spatialities of care, and longitudinal methods.

Maarja Kaaristo is based in the Department of Ethnology in the Institute for Cultural Studies and Fine Arts at the University of Tartu, Estonia.

Fabiola Mancinelli is based in the Department of Social and Cultural Anthropology at the University of Barcelona, Spain.

Lena Mortensen is based in the Department of Anthropology at the University of Toronto Scarborough, Toronto, Canada.

David Picard is an anthropologist working at the University of Lausanne, Switzerland, with research interests in tourism and travel culture, hospitality, nature conservation, science and epistemology, and winemaking. He has led research projects in the Indian Ocean, Australia, Portugal, South America, and Antarctica.

Celmara Pocock is based in the School of Arts and Communication at the University of Southern Queensland, Toowoomba, Australia.

Valerio Simoni is based at the Graduate Institute of International and Development Studies (IHEID), Switzerland.

David Trigger is based in the School of Social Science at the University of Queensland, Brisbane, Australia.

INTRODUCTION

Regimes of value in tourism

'Value' is a term frequently used in tourism studies as a measure of monetary worth, a concept governing commodity exchange, and a gauge for tourist satisfaction. However, while these dimensions of touristic value are important for understanding the economic and commercial mechanisms of tourism enterprises, they do not seem to capture the entire gamut of value's meaning when taking tourism as a social, cultural, political, and psychological phenomenon (Picard & Di Giovine, 2014; Picard & Robinson, 2012). The need for a critical exploration of value in tourism, beyond the conventional economic angle that has seen the concept regularly quantified, is evidenced by recurring debates within the field about commodification, marketing, authenticity, and the subjective experience of destinations. Tourism is a social field in which different meanings of, and ideological claims to, value become visible and often clash. Through the public display of social life, sites, and cultural artefacts, value is mobilized as a tangible resource, as an ethical claim, and as a cultural device governing tourism production. Indeed, a large number of tourism-related practices, services, and exchanges escape any strict definition of commodities, such as forms of free hospitality, sites located in the public domain, or intangible tourist values such as the perceived atmosphere of a city, beauty of a landscape or artwork, purity of a natural or spiritual site, or the relative friendliness of a local population.

 While the creation of a more inclusive, nuanced theorization of value is certainly appealing, Eiss and Pedersen (2002) warn that there is a risk of simply reproducing what they see as a number of prominent binaries that characterize the literature on the subject, in which value is described as being either about measure or meaning, quality or quantity, and objects or social relations. Instead, Eiss and Pedersen argue that 'the value of value as a theoretical concept and mode of analysis rests in its capacity to transcend such oppositions and offer a multidimensional rubric for critical transdisciplinary inquiry' (2002, p. 283). Bearing this in mind, our theoretical orientation to the question of value in tourism draws on anthropological approaches to exchange and material culture that permit us to investigate the relationships between social practices and valued objects, and the interdependencies between value as a socially or personally mutable attribute and as a calculable economic factor (Appadurai, 1986; Jamieson, 1999; Myers, 2001; Otto & Willerslev, 2013). For example, Kopytoff (1986) and Hoskins (2006) present fascinating commentaries on the entwining of people and objects whereby objects can be thought of as having histories that effectively constitute biographies and people, under particular social configurations such as slavery, can be conceptualized as taking on the properties of objects. Just as this work transcends the subject/object dichotomy, so too can meanings attached to intangible or atmospheric qualities of a tourist destination be seen as intimately linked to its measurable, economic value.

 We take the title of this special issue from Appadurai's (1986) notion of 'regimes of value', which understands value as constructed through cultural and economic processes, creating a logic of exchange and worth that can vary in its spatial extensiveness. Appadurai emphasizes that participation in a regime of value does not imply that 'every act of commodity exchange presupposes a complete cultural sharing of assumptions, but rather that the degree of value coherence may be highly variable from situation to situation' (1986, p. 15). This theorization allows us to conceptualize value as socially constructed within particular regimes, yet potentially transcendent of cultural boundaries, as demonstrated in tourism by transactions that take place between actors from different cultures. Graeber (2001) notes that the term 'regimes of value' has been popularly adopted within anthropological circles, with authors frequently adapting its meaning to suit their own arguments and theoretical proclivities. The gleaning of his terminology without subscribing precisely to Appadurai's theorization is not necessarily a problem, as Graeber acknowledges, but rather something to be aware of. We too use the term more as a source of inspiration and as a starting point for conceptualizing value differently than as a set theory to be strictly adhered to.

The plurality of regimes of value existing in any given set of practices can perhaps be best observed through the modifications that occur to material objects as they circulate through space, time and systems of meaning, as in Ateljevic and Doorne's (2003) tracing of tourism commodities from their production in China to consumption in New Zealand; a rare example of the application of these concepts to a tourism context. Appadurai argues that such circulation gives an insight into the 'social life' of objects and allows us to conceptualize 'the commodity [a]s not one kind of thing rather than another, but one phase in the life of some things' (1986, p. 17; Abram, this volume). Similarly, Cavanaugh (2007) charts the changing values of the salami produced in the Bergamo province of Northern Italy, which has evolved from a local delicacy produced on a small scale to an international commodity that attracts visitors to the region and creates lucrative exports. This transformation in the material and symbolic value of the Bergamasco salami has embroiled it in what Cavanaugh refers to as a 'tournament of value' that has brought local producers into conflict over the authenticity of their products, impacted on social networks, and called into question the basis of local identities.

To take another tourism-related example, French (1999) explores the historically changing regimes of value governing the Angkor Wat temples in Cambodia in order to understand the rampant theft of carvings and sculptures from the site. French's politicized analysis puts forward the argument that these once-sacred carvings have become reclassified as commodities, thus departing from a religious, culturally specific regime of value and becoming subsumed under one that is secular and trans-cultural (1999, p. 173). Both regimes of value are represented, at least at a rhetorical level, as incommensurable: one cannot be applied in the terms of the other. The quest for a spiritually elevated authenticity is put in antithetical terms to the acquisition of mass-produced goods – though, as the case studies in this special issue will demonstrate, both regimes are usually contextually or temporarily separated phases of a same production and consumption process. Building on this existing work within tourism studies and social anthropology, this special issue aims to make a theoretically and empirically rich contribution to the study of value in tourism. This enquiry allows us to engage with diverse topics such as how new regimes of value emerge, the role of cultural norms in the determination of value, the power dynamics and social practices at work, the impact of regimes of value on the identities and subjectivities of tourism actors, and the friction between socially held conventions about the commensurability or incommensurability of specific regimes of value related to attractions, people visited, and tourist experience.

The papers brought together in this special issue demonstrate how regimes of value in tourism can coexist, collide, and compete across a varied geographic terrain. Through the authors' careful ethnographic work we traverse five continents, presenting case studies from Australia, Madagascar, Honduras, Cuba, Estonia, and Norway. Be it in relation to value in its economic, cultural, or personal manifestation, the practices explored in these papers show that tourism not only feeds off existing conceptions of value but is also instrumental in reproducing and reinforcing regimes of value. In this sense, this special issue contributes to an emerging body of literature examining tourism's 'worldmaking' potential (Hollins-head, 2009; Hollinshead, Ateljevic, & Ali, 2009; Swain, 2009). The first three papers of this collection cohere around a central tension about the notion of pre-modernity as a trope-value for modern society, revealing regimes of value embedded in complex postco-lonial settings. By exploring the creation of value around the concepts of 'indigeneity', 'primitivity', and 'ancientness', these papers demonstrate how tourism mediates relations between culture and nature and how it impacts on popular understandings of history and temporality across various different cultures. The final three papers of this special issue examine regimes of value that implicate personal values, feelings, and relationalities between tourism actors and the landscapes that they traverse.

Contributions to the special issue

In our opening paper, David Picard, Celmara Pocock, and David Trigger analyze the social and cultural production of indigeneity in a wildlife sanctuary on the Australian Gold Coast. The sanctuary contains conventional displays of native Australian animal species – the narrative around which implies a fundamental separation between indigen-ous nature and modern human society – but is also the rather peculiar setting for a dance show regularly performed by Aboriginal people. The authors argue that this collocation symbolically creates a regime of value that subsumes Aboriginal people under the cat-egory of indigenous nature; an arrangement that has potentially troubling socio-political implications by way of its apparent ontological separation between 'White' and 'Black' Australians.

In a similar vein, Fabiola Mancinelli explores the social valorization of the intangible resource of 'primitiveness' through an analysis of tourism mediators' discourses around the Zafimaniry – a remote community of swidden cultivators and woodcarvers living in the mountains of central Madagascar. She argues that the Zafimaniry are valorized and framed by a 'primitivist narrative' that simultaneously evokes in Western tourists a sense of imperialist nostalgia for a seemingly ancient, vanishing way of life and a philanthropic attitude in response to the villagers' extreme poverty. Through what she refers to as a 'poetics of time', Mancinelli explores how both Western and local Malagasy tourism actors position the Zafimaniry as pre-modern cultural relics to be gazed upon. This clearly parallels Picard, Pocock, and Trigger's elucidation of the symbolic embedding of Aboriginal people within a romanticized landscape of indigenous, pre-modern nature in the context of the Australian wildlife sanctuary.

We then turn to Lena Mortensen's assessment of the branding mechanisms at work in Copán, Honduras, where the maintenance and reproduction of the 'ancient Maya' brand have opened up a lucrative tourism market. Her analysis traces the conversion of symbolic value associated with the archaeological site into economic value through the work of branding and tourism initiatives. Mortensen shows how international interest in the heritage site has created an impetus for local communities to conform to the ancient Maya brand, for example through painting their houses in specially selected brand colours, in order to reap the benefits of such fervent tourist attention. While at the local level, it appears that a brand-ing synergy is at least possible, the paper also explores the difficulty of aligning the Copán

Maya brand with Honduran nation-branding and the tendency for the political present of the country to be elided in touristic representations of a timeless, stylized past.

Shifting to the special issue's second thematic cluster, Simone Abram's paper contributes an insightful and original look at the multiple forms of value invested in traditional Norwegian holiday homes. Abram describes the significance of these rural cabins as places that Norwegian families use to congregate and share leisure time, but which also bind family members together legally through a complex system of partible inheritance and part-ownership. As a result, kinship relations are partly inscribed through family members' ownership of shares in these holiday homes, resulting in connections that are reliant on economic, legal, and relational/emotional regimes of value – regimes that can come into conflict when families dispute the fate of a cabin.

Maarja Kaaristo presents a fascinating study of the regulation of aural environments on rural Estonian tourist farms. Through her sensitive ethnographic work, Kaaristo shows how 'peace and quiet' is not a given feature of the countryside but instead forms part of a socially constructed 'rural sound idyll' that is harnessed by farmers as a form of value to attract tourists, but which also arises as a potential source of conflict with visitors. Rather than pandering to their every desire, the Estonian tourism farmers encourage their guests to share their appreciation and respect for the serenity of the surrounding nature, for example by not playing loud music or letting off fireworks. Kaaristo's research is intriguing in the way that it elucidates the embodied, sensory dimension of value creation and through its close attention to the deeply held personal values that impact on broader value creation in tourism.

In a continuation of this relational theme, Valerio Simoni takes us on a journey through the streets of Havana where he vividly describes the interactions, identifications, and intimacies that take place between foreign tourists and local Cubans. He explains how the friendly advances of locals are often mistrusted by tourists, who perceive the Cubans as being insincere, 'deceptive hustlers' who are more interested in making financial gains than initiating real friendships or relationships. In this context of suspicion, Simoni suggests that intimacy arises as a regime of value determining an aspiration, shared by the tourists and locals, to be treated as unique individuals and united by their common humanity.

References

Appadurai, A. (1986). Introduction: Commodities and the politics of value. In A. Appadurai (Ed.), *The social life of things* (pp. 3–63). Cambridge: Cambridge University Press.

Ateljevic, I., & Doorne, S. (2003). Culture, economy and tourism commodities: Social relations of production and consumption. *Tourist Studies, 3*(2), 123–141.

Cavanaugh, J. R. (2007). Making salami, producing Bergamo: The transformation of value. *Ethnos: Journal of Anthropology, 72*(2), 149–172.

Eiss, P. K., & Pedersen, D. (2002). Introduction: Values of value. *Cultural Anthropology, 17*(3), 283–290.

French, L. (1999). Hierarchies of value at Angkor Wat. *Ethnos: Journal of Anthropology, 64*(2), 170–191.

Graeber, D. (2001). *Toward an anthropological theory of value: The false coin of our own dreams.* New York, NY: Palgrave.

Hollinshead, K. (2009). The "worldmaking" prodigy of tourism: The reach and power of tourism in the dynamics of change and transformation. *Tourism Analysis, 14*(1), 139–152.

Hollinshead, K., Ateljevic, I., & Ali, N. (2009). Worldmaking agency–worldmaking authority: The sovereign constitutive role of tourism. *Tourism Geographies, 11*(4), 427–443.

Hoskins, J. (2006). Agency, biography and objects. In C. Tilley, W. Keane, S. Kuchler, M. Rowlands, & P. Spitzer (Eds.), *Handbook of material culture* (pp. 74–84). London: Sage.

Jamieson, M. (1999). The place of counterfeits in regimes of value: An anthropological approach. *The Journal of the Royal Anthropological Institute*, *5*(1), 1–11.

Kopytoff, I. (1986). The cultural biography of things: Commoditization as process. In A. Appadurai (Ed.), *The social life of things* (pp. 64–91). Cambridge: Cambridge University Press.

Myers, F. R. (2001). Introduction: The Empire of things. In F. R. Myers (Ed.), *The empire of things: Regimes of value and material culture* (pp. 3–64). Oxford: James Curry.

Otto, T., & Willerslev, R. (2013). Introduction: 'Value as theory': Comparison, cultural critique, and guerilla ethnographic theory. *HAU: Journal of Ethnographic Theory*, *3*(1), 1–20.

Picard, D., & Di Giovine, M. (Eds.). (2014). *Tourism and the power of otherness*. Clevedon: Channel View.

Picard, D., & Robinson, M. (Eds.). (2012). *Emotion in motion: Tourism, affect and transformation*. London: Ashgate.

Swain, M. B. (2009). The cosmopolitan hope of tourism: Critical action and worldmaking vistas. *Tourism Geographies*, *11*(4), 505–525.

Dr Émilie Crossley
Dr David Picard

Tourism as theatre: performing and consuming indigeneity in an Australian wildlife sanctuary

David Picard[a], Celmara Pocock[b] and David Trigger[c]

[a]CEG/IGOT-Universidade de Lisboa, Lisbon, Portugal; [b]School of Arts and Communication, University of Southern Queensland, Toowoomba, QLD, Australia; [c]School of Social Science, The University of Queensland, Brisbane, QLD, Australia

This article explores the social and cultural production of indigeneity in a wildlife sanctuary on the Australian Gold Coast. We note that the human and animal characters that form the displays of the sanctuary work towards the assemblage of a largely consistent underlying theme. The latter reproduces commensurability between two main figures associated with Australian settler history, namely the country's pre-colonial indigenous species of animals and plants and the human Aboriginal population. We argue that the theatre produced in the park's highly sanitized visitor contact zone has wider social and political ramifications for Australian society and modern society in general. By ceremonially re-enacting the historical myth of separation between modern civilization and primordial indigeneity, through a tourist enterprise, the sanctuary produces ambivalent meanings about the relation between 'nativeness' in nature and society. Our analysis addresses the simultaneous emancipation of contemporary human indigeneity as a revitalized cultural value together with the social distancing of Aboriginal people as one-dimensional caricatures of primordial nature.

Introduction

In the early 1940s, Alex Griffiths, a beekeeper and flower grower living in the coastal town of Currumbin on Queensland's Gold Coast in eastern Australia saw swarms of wild lorikeets ravaging his fields. Lorikeets are small arboreal parrots characterized by their special-ized brush-tipped tongues for feeding on nectar of blossoms and soft fruits.[1] To lure the birds away from his fields, Griffiths started to feed them with a mixture of milk, water and sugar. His strategy worked and his feeding sessions started to attract hundreds of birds. Early images of such sessions show Griffiths literally within a cloud of lorikeets, sitting on his arms, head and shoulders (Figure 1).

At that time, in the years following the end of World War II, Queensland's Gold Coast had started to transform into one of Australia's largest coastal resort clusters. Once the tour-ists and tourist agents got wind of the lorikeet feeding, the Currumbin location began to attract ever-increasing numbers of visitors. In 1947, Griffiths established Currumbin Bird Sanctuary, to better organize the setting for visitors who wanted to witness and assist the feeding sessions. Over the following years, the sanctuary started to accommodate other

GOOD LUCK!
FROM —
THE SANCTUARY
CURRUMBIN BEACH. QLD.

Figure 1.   Alex Griffiths, founder of Currumbin, with lorikeets. Kodak postcard c.1938. Reproduced with kind permission of the Centre for the Government of Queensland, The University of Queensland.

types of animals. It gradually developed into a large zoological garden priding itself on being home to one of the most substantial collections of Australian native wildlife in the world. It became a National Trust of Queensland property in 1976 and was renamed Currumbin Wildlife Sanctuary in 1995. Through the employment of experienced zoo managers and wildlife keepers during the 1990s and 2000s, the sanctuary's management and curatorial work were progressively professionalized.

In a context marked by stiff economic competition with other Queensland zoos and Gold Coast tourism attractions, the sanctuary developed a differentiation strategy based on providing an 'Australian' experience to both domestic visitors and international tourists. While building new attractions and developing innovations in recent years, the sanctuary remains committed to the theme of 'Australianness' and 'bushiness', to quote an ex-Chief Executive Officer interviewed in 2007. Animal displays were re-arranged to foreground enigmatic species native to different parts of the Australian continent (only some of which were endemic to the region of Currumbin's location), including koalas, Tasmanian devils, crocodiles, various large birds, snakes, kangaroos and so on. Many of these animals were purposefully 'conditioned' – a term used by the zookeepers – in order to provide a tourist display. Koalas, for instance, are said to undergo several years of training before they could accept being touched and 'hugged' by tourists as part of a photo shoot. The Sanctuary website asserts that 'all of our koalas are conditioned from a young age to feel comfortable around humans'.[2] Since the 1990s, a wildlife hospital funded through donations became a major new income provider as well as a successful public relations vehicle focused on 'many feel-good stories' according to our ex-CEO interviewee. The slogan of the sanctuary was changed to 'More Australian, More Natural, More Fun', hence emphasizing the indigenous nature of the sanctuary's displays.

In 2004, a troupe performing Aboriginal and Torres Strait Islander dances and songs was integrated into the sanctuary's programme of exhibits. Since the end of that decade, the dance troupe started to offer a separate evening programme, introducing paying tourists to selected accounts of Aboriginal history and culture. Tourists could thus experience the performance of producing and consuming a dinner incorporating foods cooked using an adaptation of the traditional ground oven known most widely by the north Australian Torres Strait Islands term *kup-murri*.

Currumbin Wildlife Sanctuary provides an interesting case illustrating how different figures and narratives about wildlife, nature and indigeneity can converge in an overarching plot and play. It challenges in particular questions about the production of value in tourism. If most tourism economists approach such value in terms of quantitatively measurable expenditure and income, generated in particular by the hospitality, transport and entertainment industries, this form of analysis can only poorly capture the wider regimes of value that govern touristic encounters and contact zones. Social scientists including Nash (1977), MacCannell (1976) and Lash and Urry (1994) have long pointed out that tourism is governed above all by an economy based on the production of signs and site-based attractions. The provision of secure and often highly standardized basic infrastructures, such as hotels, restaurants, hospitals and transport facilities, usually functions merely as a baseline necessity, but not, in most cases, as an attraction in itself. There are exceptions where hotels or purpose-built leisure parks are at the same time the major attractions, as in the cases of iconic facilities in Dubai or America's Disneyworld, and indeed in several Australian Gold Coast theme parks. However, in most cases, a large part of the value produced and consumed in tourist attractions is found outside these basic infrastructures. The study of value in tourism hence needs to embrace a more encompassing scope of inquiry exploring different concomitant regimes of value and their entanglements.

One way to respond to this challenge is to conceptualize tourism in terms of a highly theatrical social play where various actors take up roles and act out scripts. This approach follows the Canadian sociologist Goffman (1959) who worked brilliantly to understand how people engage in routine interactions with others. In most everyday life-contexts, including tourism, there is no fixed setting, as in a conventional theatre where the stage is redecorated for each successive act. Instead, social actors move through different locales that are organized and bound by specific socially construed rules of engagement and interaction rituals (Goffman, 1959), meta-narratives (Bruner & Kirshenblatt-Gimblett, 1994) or indeed forms of plot (Picard & Zuev, 2014).

The epistemic strategy of approaching tourism through the concept of theatrical play hence is to follow the sequences of actual events and settings experienced by tourists, rather than the multiplicity of personal tastes, motivations and travel modes of individuals that might be elicited through interviews and surveys (Edensor, 2000; Picard, 2012, 2013). In a place like Currumbin, Australia, invariably visitors enter through a main gate, and mostly experience the suite of attractions of the park in a broadly similar sequential order, subtly governed by the spatial arrangements and the timetable of advertised stage performances that include animal feedings and the Aboriginal dance presentation.

Put in this context, the sanctuary and its different site-based attractions become the specific settings for the wider play and plot of, as advertised by the park, Australian indigenous nature that visitors engage in both as spectators and as participating actors. This article explores this performance both in terms of the figures and sign-worlds staged in the wildlife sanctuary and the exchanges of meanings operated in and beyond its different settings. We are particularly interested in the ambivalence of the sign-value of indigeneity produced through the sanctuary's displays and what it can tell us in a wider sense about Australian contemporary society and modernity at large. We have carried out empirical research in relation to the park in 2007 and 2012, combining direct observations of the displays on three occasions with desktop research (examining historical data, advertisement brochures and park internal strategy documents), formal interviews with several of the sanctuary's main stakeholders and (human) performers, and several informal conversations with staff and visitors at the park.

Design of the staged settings

Currumbin Wildlife Sanctuary is entered through a main gate leading into a wide-open square, bound by several buildings and a fenced-off area used for feeding the lorikeets. The site opens at 8 am and visitors gather in the patio area, which is accessible free of charge, while awaiting the bird-feeding spectacle. Several keepers then appear holding small buckets filled with a watery sweet liquid. Immediately, several dozen lorikeets fly towards each of them, landing on their arms, shoulders and heads, trying to get some of the sweet mixture into their beaks. Other lorikeets perch on the metal structures installed inside the fenced area including two large spinning wheels that start to twirl under the weight of the birds. Visitors are invited to take turns in holding the feeding plates so that they too become immersed in clouds of the colourful little animals. Lots of noises, squealing, yelping and shouting are heard, and many photos are taken (Figure 2).

At the conclusion of the bird feeding in the open access area, some visitors leave the sanctuary, while others purchase an entry ticket to the main park. Currumbin Wildlife Sanctuary has a total size of 27 hectares and is organized in several spatially discrete thematic sections. Visitors enter through a relatively large souvenir shop that is predominantly a timber structure painted on the outside with the distinctive patterns of Aboriginal art (Figure 3). A large sign on one of the walls reads: 'The Spirit of the Outback'. Indirect warm light illuminates the interior and its sales displays. During most of the day identifiably Aboriginal music is played, often featuring the now iconic

Figure 2.   A keeper and visitors feeding lorikeets. © Celmara Pocock, 2012.

Figure 3.   Entrance to the Currumbin Wildlife Sanctuary. © David Picard, 2012.

didgeridoo.[3] Amidst a wide range of souvenirs available for purchase are miniature representations of both native animals and human Aboriginal figurines in close proximity on certain shelves (Figure 4).

Once visitors pass through the souvenir shop-entrance, they arrive in a small square that has a mini-train station located on its perimeter. To get from here to the other main area of the park one needs to pass through a tunnel, either on foot or by taking the mini-train. The inside of the tunnel is painted in bright colours suggesting a spatially condensed traverse of Australia from coast to coast through the desert-like wilderness of the Outback (but not through any form of city or other sign of human modern life). The mini-train allows visitors to move through the entire park, running in a continuous loop, and stopping at all major visitor locales (Figure 5).

The park includes two open-air amphitheatres used for animal shows, one called 'close encounters' mainly involving supervised contact with snakes, the other a flying show with various native birds. It also includes an indoor cinema-style theatre where films about the sanctuary are continuously screened. Adjacent to the children's playground, and of considerable significance in our analysis, Aboriginal dancers perform on a sandy ground next to a tented area. This is the only form of performance focused on human culture across the 'wildlife' sanctuary's displays of non-human animal behaviours and characteristics.

At various points inside the park signposts indicate directions to the different areas and attractions (Figure 6). The architecture of the park does not appear to follow a linear or other systematic pattern. Instead the arrangement of the different locales appears unstructured. Visitors are not given clear indication to guide them through the park in a particular sequence. In that sense, visitors are invited to stroll around the park, choosing their own itineraries and perhaps getting lost, thus discovering the different displays and arrangements

Figure 4.   Miniature native animals and human Aboriginal figurines in close proximity in the souve-nir shop. © David Trigger, 2007.

as if accidentally. However, the tight-knit programme of feeding and animal-show sessions ensures that many visitors follow similar itineraries, and as evident in our brief observations, at times rush from one display or feeding show to the other.

Aboriginal dance performance attraction

The 'Aboriginal dance show' is accommodated in a tent and open sandy arena near the first train stop beyond the tunnel and close to the children's island playground (Figure 5). This performance concludes the daily programme of shows and attractions. It is opened by a

Figure 5.   Site map of Currumbin Wildlife Sanctuary. Photographed by Celmara Pocock, 2012.

young man sitting on the ground playing a didgeridoo, a musical instrument which though not used or produced traditionally in this region of eastern Australia, has become a nationally and internationally significant cultural emblem of Aboriginal culture (Neuenfeldt, 1997). A moderator, one of the dance company's directors, explains via loudspeaker that this is a 'Didgeridoo blessing' and the ensuing dances are ways to contact the performers' ancestors, to ask for permission to receive the visitors in the grounds and to seek protection for them. He announces that there will be a photo opportunity after the show.

A group of five young men then enters the sandy ground. All are barefoot, with bare torsos and their skin painted with rough white stripes. Basic clap stick rhythms and the vibrating sounds of the didgeridoo drive the dances, which are performed through stomping movements of the feet, flowing ecstatic motions of the body and rhythmic singing of short verses or words. Visitors get progressively involved, mainly by being invited to repeat certain rhymes or words, and clapping in the rhythm of the music. Once the performance ends, visitors are invited to join the dancers for the taking of photos (Figure 7). Prior to this invitation, visitors are requested not to take photographs, as the dances are regarded as 'sacred' by the moderator.

This human performance inside a wildlife park seems somewhat uncanny, if not dis-placed, at a time when post-settler countries like Australia seek to accord equal citizenship to Aboriginal people and ensure broadly respectful recognition of Indigenous culture (cf. Bunten, 2014). For such human displays, or perhaps displays of humans, coterminous with presentations of other species in nature, might well be regarded as resembling colonial world fairs and zoological exhibitions during the nineteenth and early twentieth centuries.

Figure 6.   Signpost Directing Visitors to the Park's Attractions. © David Picard, 2012.

In denouncing past treatment of Aboriginal people there is recognition of inappropriate con-flation of the Indigenous population with flora and fauna in public discourses and legis-lation.[4] Indeed, the current CEO interviewed in 2012 noted the risk of 'tokenism' if the Aboriginal presence becomes a kind of 'poster child' to sell the theme of Australian nature in the park. This is particularly so, he said, when in fact there is only a minor con-tribution of the Aboriginal performers to the overall operation of the Wildlife Sanctuary. Our research sought, in part, to address this issue through discussions with members of the Aboriginal dance group.

    Yanguwah, which is the name of the dance company, was run by a male/female couple, both of mixed Indigenous/Euro-Australian ancestry. They explained that each of them had been raised with little influence from Aboriginal culture. During our April 2012 interview,

Figure 7.   Photos with the Members of the Indigenous Dance Group (D. Picard and C. Pocock shown as visitors). © Catarina Moreira, 2012.

the couple explained that they 'rediscovered' their Indigenous heritage only later in life. During the 1980s, the man was trained as a cultural performer and dancer at the Aboriginal and Islander Dance Theatre (AIDT, later renamed NAISDA, National Aboriginal and Islander Skills Development Association) in the Australian city of Sydney. The dance school was created in the 1970s, under the leadership of an African-American dancer, Carole Johnson, who toured Australia and then relocated from America to lead a programme of development in Australian Indigenous dance (DeFrantz, 2011, pp. 60–61; Walker, 2010, p. 40; see also Robinson, 2000). This was a form of postcolonial cultural revival achieved in part by mobilizing, through performance, a popular imaginary about an ancestral Aboriginal cosmology. The latter being a spiritual worldview based upon the notion of a primordial 'Dreamtime', during which land, people and the universe, and the relations between these were formed.

While there has been a debate as to the mix of Indigenous cultural traditions and Euro-Australian desires that have likely informed the development of this idea of an Aboriginal spirituality focused on the Dreaming (Langton & David, 2003; Merlan, 1997; Waitt, 1999; Wolfe, 1991, 1994), there is little argument that it is now a widespread signifier for the celebration and recuperation of Australian Aboriginal indigeneity. The case of the Currumbin dance group seems to clearly illustrate the presentation of Indigenous spirituality for consumption by a public receptive to the identification of Aboriginal people with the romance of nature evident in both the totemic precepts of the Dreaming and more broadly in the nativeness of the continent's wildlife (cf. Waitt, 1999).

The couple directing the dance company in the Currumbin Wildlife Sanctuary explained that they met one another at an Aboriginal dance performance show in the Northern Queensland resort town of Cairns. He was from the Gold Coast area in the south of the State and she was from the Torres Strait Islands in the north. They moved to Currumbin in the 2000s, after arranging a contract with the Sanctuary, which they believe gave them substantial financial and programmatic autonomy. From the early 2010s, an evening programme was added as an extension to the Currumbin daytime schedule. Here visitors arrive in the Sanctuary through a separate entrance leading to an inside bar and lounge. They are welcomed by two young women in stylized Pacific Islander dress and invited to enjoy drinks before the start of the show. As part of the first act, the visitors are asked to enter a small lecture theatre, where one of the company directors welcomes them and gives a lecture in two parts. The lecture concerns Australian Indigenous people's histories and possible futures. The first part is called 'dispossession' and the second 'reconciliation'. The lecture is accompanied by a selection of images projected onto a wall; the first part mainly in black and white depicting historical violence towards Indigenous people and the second in colour showing figures and scenes of reconciliation, such as Aboriginal and Euro-Australian children playing together, mixed couples and Aboriginal persons in successful roles.

As a means to integrate the visitors into the performance, one member of the audience is appointed to be the *Bala* who, according to the explanation given, is a warrior and messenger who will look after the other visitors.[5] The visitors are then asked to go outside into the park, traverse the before-mentioned tunnel and meet a group of young men (the same that performed the dance in the afternoon) at a small house. The men cook food (meat and vegetables) in a ground oven which, with the help of the *Bala* and other visitors, is uncovered by removing coals and hot stones. After further performed ceremonial actions (to request from the spiritual world hospitality, to announce peaceful intentions of the humans present and so on), the visitors sit down on wooden benches inside a half-open tent.

Explanations similar to those during the afternoon are given via loudspeaker and a series of dances are performed. Later the food is blessed and God is thanked indicating the mix of Christian and Aboriginal cosmological ideas informing the performance (cf. Magowan, 2000). The dancers initially wear attire similar to that worn during the afternoon show, while at a later stage of the evening programme they get changed and reappear wearing the feather headdress, or *dhari*, of Torres Strait Islander culture.[6] It is explained to the visitors that the first series of dances are 'sacred' Aboriginal dances, prohibited to be filmed or photographed. The second series are adaptations from Torres Strait Islander (Melanesian) dances, and are more jovial and playful and visitors are invited to join in and make recordings. The show ends, once again, in a photo-taking session.

Figurations and character traits of Australia's indigenous nature

If the overall theme of the Wildlife Sanctuary is Australian indigenous nature, this concept itself becomes a figure in a literal or theatrical sense, re-appearing through the orally performed discourses of both the wildlife keepers and human Indigenous performers. This is reiterated in the visual pictograms and written explanations that are placed throughout the Sanctuary. The performances and texts reveal the discursive formation of Australian indigeneity as a specific form of uncanny nature, socially distanced from the modern life embodied by tourist visitors, yet also the focus of a desire to be intimately close to the cultural values of nativeness and naturalness.

In relation to nativeness in nature, a major character trait associated with this expression of indigeneity is that of 'toughness'. Virtually all displays or explanations about wild animals or natural environments a visitor encounters in the Sanctuary stress this specific quality. To survive, one either has to be as tough as this wild nature or, alternatively, develop smart skills. At the crocodile cages, a loudspeaker explains that in this natural world, 'you are either prey or hunter'. Different animals function here as dramatic characters that mediate and ultimately play out these two strategies. One category of animals comprises the dominant aggressive species at the head of the food chain. This category is associated with the role of hunter and is stronger than all others – not only in terms of survival, but also in terms of capacity to mate and reproduce. The zookeeper at the dingo cage explains that relations within species are ruled by the same principles; in the wild, the group is headed by an alpha-male.

The second category of animal-figures encountered at the zoo is defined by cleverness and degree of ingenuity. These are often physically weaker, smaller animals that possess passive defensive strategies, hiding and tricking the hunters through cunning forms of camouflage or creating smart protective shields. A widely mediated example is the case of the echidnas rolling up their bodies into a ball of spikes. Another smart strategy mediated through the animal displays is for a species to scare or poison physically dominant animals. A large part of the discourses about snakes at the 'Close Encounter' display, for instance, focuses on their variable degrees of venomousness, explaining in each case how a human would die after being bitten.

While the discourses of the wildlife sanctuary displays mainly emphasize aggressive relations between species, and among males within species, in an apparent counterpoint, the relations between adults and offspring are mostly portrayed as caring, or even 'family oriented'. The echidnas lay eggs, yet still feed their young with milk and hence, despite their prickly appearance reveal themselves as soft and caring parents. The same applies for the crocodile females who are presented as gentle and even tender mothers. There is a degree of anthropomorphism evident in this type of discourse.

In this sense, the overall 'logic' presented as governing the realm of Australian indigenous nature is to survive and reproduce. A discourse recorded on several occasions in the sanctuary stresses that in this context 'deficient animals' are 'weeded out' which 'generates a natural balance based upon a healthy ecosystem'. One senior keeper, responsible for the dingo cage, explains that these animals 'have been around for 4,000 years, are predators and top of the food chain, therefore the managers of nature; they control populations and weed out deficient animals and keep ecosystems healthy'.[7] A similar commentary can be heard during the bird flight show, stressing the natural balance of wild environments, where one either adapts or gets eaten.

Most of this rhetoric stresses that once humans intervene, this natural balance gets disturbed, and a form of native sustainability is lost. In the case of the dingo, once it is hunted by smart humans it loses its role as the top predator responsible for keeping ecosystems in good shape. In this sense, human interventions are defined as destabilizing what is imagined as a prior ideal state (cf. Rose, 1997), potentially creating instead forms of instability. The logical ambiguity of excluding humans from 'natural' native nature in this type of discourse has been critiqued in both the natural and social sciences (Mulcock & Trigger, 2008). Furthermore, there is ambiguity as to whether Aboriginal hunters are included as destabilizing native nature or whether this outcome is confined to the majority of the national population seemingly understood as more 'modern' than those who identify as Indigenous. The inclusion of human indigeneity in the park alongside idealized native species would suggest the presumption that Aboriginal people are not a threat to nature because they are themselves 'native'. However, the discourses of nativeness in nature and society respectively, are inconsistent on this issue; wildlife officers present indigeneity in nature, while Aboriginal performers articulate indigeneity among humans, and there are both overlaps and oppositions in these respective displays.

This exploration of character traits associated with Australian indigenous nature, mediated through the different animal displays in the sanctuary, demonstrates a conception of a magical, wonderful world in perpetual balance, with its own laws and logics, outside modern human experience and life. It emerges as akin to earlier pre-modernist and modernist imaginaries of a primordial wild nature located in the past of such settler societies as Australia (for a wider range of cases, cf. Picard & Di Giovine, 2014). Such imaginaries have been contextually adapted and mediated by romanticist painters such as Tom Roberts, Frederick McCubbin, Charles Condor, Hans Heysen and Arthur Streeton, who produced highly popular colourful impressions of the country's nature found in the bush and outback (McLean, 1998, 2003; White, 1981, pp. 86–87). They seem to have contributed to the formation of a national imagery that finds in a specific conception of indigenous nature a metaphorical focus point; an *ur*-condition from which the colonial enterprise of settling and inhabiting Australia was started. As we will argue, indigenous human populations are here widely assimilated to this *ur*-nature, which contributes to the contemporary ambivalence of their identity as understood across Australian society.

At the same time, indigenous nature supplies a parable to think about the order underlying human life in general. It is delineated by broadly assumed discourses which find in the taming of this nature a common ground, a resource and rationale for national identity, if not a reason for being. Maintaining difference with and distance from nature while ceremonially appropriating its presumed essence is simultaneously a means to reaffirm and reconstitute a particular type of modern national self (cf. Graburn, 2013).

Indigenous nature and culture as ontologically discrete

If the spaces and displays staged in Currumbin Wildlife Sanctuary form a specific type of theatrical setting, the visitor is attributed a particular role within the wider play that unfolds. He or she is challenged to take on the role of what in a classical theatrical setting would be the main character, or hero, whose sequence of encounters and adventures bring the story forward. In this sense, through this projection, the visitors become part of the wider stage settings and story. From the moment they enter the area of the sanctuary, they become in a way mini-heroes immersing themselves in the realms of a wild indigenous nature. The zookeepers act here as a type of guide-figure helping them through the challenges they meet on their way.

A dominant discourse performed in the zoo is that humans, while in one sense outside of native nature, when entering its world encounter it as an equal. This is because humans are presented as another species of animal. This, it is stressed, makes such encounters, *a priori*, a dangerous enterprise both for the humans and, as we will show further, for the animals. Like the animals, in order to survive the humans have to be tough, skilled and smart. They have to know what to avoid, for example, crocodiles and their habitat, the coastal estuaries of northern Australia. They have to be smart not to get bitten by a snake by remaining calm in the presence of such a dangerous reptile and avoiding contact. Alternatively, humans have to be categorized as hunters rather than as prey. At the half island inside the lake, there are children's playground installations simulating a spider web. Kids are invited to climb onto these and train their sense of balance. A loudspeaker voice challenges them, asking: 'are you brave enough to play with the spider net? Use your skills and strength to escape one of nature's deadliest traps'.

And, in relation to risks of disease or infection potentially present in Australian nature, the zoo systematically recommends a strict hygiene protocol. After each potential contact with animals, visitors are encouraged to wash their hands, for instance after the photo sessions with a baby crocodile, a possum, snakes or a koala. While these precautions have a concrete purpose to avoid bacterial contaminations, they also reinforce the sense of a need to keep the two worlds of modern humans and wild nature separate. Paying customers are constantly reminded that they are only visitors to a world that is fundamentally different. Protected by a host of security measures – disinfectant gels, protective barriers and walls, glass cages, water channels – they can temporarily enter nature, but they must eventually return and thus reaffirm a profound ontological separation between human society and the domain of the indigenous wild.

We have addressed how this nature is denoted through a set of character traits which formulate it as a tough and dangerous realm. Yet once this domain of the wild is put in contrast to the world of modern human society those characteristics are transformed. Native nature becomes a world radically different, a place seemingly of mystical powers and knowledge, filled with gruesome beings talented with subtle sensory faculties: crocodiles, for example, that feel the presence of others through their indistinct vibrations; pelicans that predict when floods are to occur; shy snakes that avoid conflict at all costs and will rather flee. While tough, indigenous nature is simultaneously portrayed as vulnerable and, in a way, innocent in that violence only occurs for a purpose. Children, one zookeeper stresses, are naturally unafraid of the creatures like snakes that inhabit this world; in the view of this person, they are not scared because they naturally know that snakes do not attack humans, and only bite by accident. Being child-like is thus stylized as a synonym for being naturally wild.

As evident at Currumbin Wildlife Sanctuary, many of the explanations given about human impacts on Australia's wildlife push the logic of the meaning of indigenous nature even further. The presence of modern human society is here repeatedly explained as a factor of decadence now distant from an initial natural state of harmony and equilibrium. Visitors not only learn that cars kill birds and other wildlife, and that deforestation, agriculture and urbanization change habitats, but also that the animals introduced by humans disturb an ecosystem that previously evolved within a state of primal harmony. The dingo and foxes, for instance, brought to Australia by humans, manage to 'open' and kill the previously perfectly protected echidnas rolled in its spiky ball. Just why killing for food is regarded as disturbance of nature remains somewhat unclear. In another case, a keeper explained that the one 'pure white' dingo that lives in the park should, in principle and by nature, be the alpha male or top dog of the group. Yet, it finds itself at the lowest rank because the other males, who are the product of interbreeding with domestic dogs, work together against the white dingo. In this case, once again, apart from whether this notion of expected dominance has any basis in the study of animal behaviour, we find the assumption that human interference in the natural order of dingo life represents a disturbance leading to a reversal of a presumed natural order.

Further, the visitors learn that because of interbreeding with domestic dogs imported from Europe, there are hardly any pure dingoes left in Australia. Here again, human action is presented as leading to decadence from a previously pure condition, this fall from natural nobility embodied in the figure of the dingo. The paradox, as with the issue of human hunting, is that the dingo was itself imported by Aboriginal people. At one time, this animal becomes a narrative figure to illustrate decadence (evident from the situation where it can kill echidnas that were previously able to defend themselves from pre-dators); while on other occasions the dingo is spoken of as *de facto* indigenized, and the embodiment of a pure primordial nature (Peace, 2001; Trigger, Mulcock, Gaynor, & Toussaint, 2008, pp. 1279–1281).

Many explanations usually presented in the second or concluding parts of zookeeper discourses deal with human impacts. A strong emphasis is put here on the transformations of natural habitats and the ensuing competition between human and natural worlds over such spaces. Visitors are told at the bird flight show that some species are not doing so well, particularly where their habitat is transformed into agricultural fields. Pelicans, for instance, rely on the flooding of plains and the subsequent abundance of food to survive. They have breeding grounds to which they return, mate, breed, raise their young and then move to other areas. Yet, the bird-guide explains that, pelicans and humans use the same water. Humans leave rubbish behind, like fishing hooks or plastic bags, which threaten the survival of these animals.

During the flight bird show, one zookeeper expresses this general argument as follows: 'Where you find humans, you find filth'. Some animals adapt to this, some – pigeons, for example – even clean up and do well. But others suffer. An indigenous wedge tailed eagle is brought in. The moderator explains that it used to be persecuted by European settlers in Australia as it was thought to attack young domesticated livestock: 'Farmers used to shoot them and almost wiped out the species'. Hence: 'we are the biggest threat; we brought in new animal predators, cars that kill many birds on the roadside'. 'Every minute, rainforest with a surface equal to 20 football fields is burned down, we build houses and leave rubbish'. In conclusion to the display, some solutions are suggested in terms of what modern humans should do: 'use and plant native trees' and 'clean up after yourself'. To reinforce the point, examples are given of positive human actions, such as the hospital initiative of the park, where injured wild animals are taken, treated and eventually released back into nature.

Wild nature hence appears as a timeless, pre-modern state subjected to the dangers of pollution and impurity emanating from the presence of modern human society. As if history only began with the first settlers arriving in Australia, the story of this indigenous wilderness might be seen as a projection of the biblical turning point of Adam and Eve being expelled from the Garden of Eden. History emerges as a progressive dilution from a presumed primordial natural state. It leads to the alteration of an initially pure and innocent nature. At the same time, in the Australian post-settler context, it seems societal reflection about the experiences of colonial history produces a new logic for action, a moral liability to preserve and protect, even rejuvenate and recreate nature in its authentic form.

Wildlife tourism as theatre: dramatizing indigeneity as the counterpoint to modern society

Through their discourses and displays, the Indigenous people performing in the park position themselves in a mediating role between modern society and native nature. Many aspects of their performances claim an ancestral incorporation into the world of nature, where human relations among them and with all other species were 'marked by peaceful harmony, the absence of violence and mutual respect' (comments repeated by the Aboriginal performers during the afternoon and evening shows). One killed an animal only if one needed to eat and asked for forgiveness. Yet, one never killed out of pleasure nor hunted game for the sake of fun.

This mediating role performed in the Sanctuary points to a wider ambivalence about the participation of Indigenous people in Australian contemporary society. When asked why they would perform alongside the displays of wild animals, one of the directors explained that 'we are a dying race, like the animals that need to be preserved'. In this sense, the indigenous human population is symbolically and ontologically assimilated to the realm of a pre-colonial native wilderness, 'perfectly adapted and skilled to survive in Australian nature' (quoted from an interview with the dance troupe director), the top of the food chain. The discourse is not new and appears to embrace an earlier nineteenth century romantic colonial perspective of the noble savage, 'closer to nature than to culture', and therefore 'doomed' to disappear within agricultural and industrial modernism (Langton, 1996).

In the assumptions underlying this discourse, the Indigenous human population, similar to the wider realm of indigenous wilderness, is seen as defenceless and subject to the aggression, contaminations and dispossession that accompanied the colonial invasion from Europe. Threatened with extinction, with their 'habitat' so radically changed, those now identifying as descended from Aboriginal or Torres Strait Islander forebears may no longer survive through future generations.

However, just as with the wider realm of wild nature, the performances about Aboriginal and Torres Strait Islander cultures and people projects the idea of a strong 'surviving spirituality', that like a small yet persisting flame continues an authentic link between the realms of primordial ancestry and Indigenous populations today. The latter, so visitors to the Currumbin Indigenous dances learn, have kept alive some primordial magic and spirituality that continues an intimate link with the wild yet captive nature put on display at the Sanctuary. To this extent, what many refer to as 'White' and 'Black' Australia hence appear to be kept in ontologically separate realms; the most stark contrast indicating a child-like 'Black' Australia, with persistent magical or spiritual ties to the land, looked after by a modern paternalistic 'White' nation-state.

In other countries with a similar demographic history, for example, Brazil or La Reunion, one can observe the claim to similar magical or spiritual ties between the land and its first populations. Yet, in these countries, the ties and the power or magic they are said to incorporate are practically dissolved into a wider national body. The national story is here less one of a quest for purity and authenticity in nature than one of accepting that social life is in perpetual transformation and creolization (Picard, 2010, 2011). Our study of a particular Australian setting suggests that the intellectual positioning of the idea of indigeneity is different. The involvement of an Indigenous performance group in a Wildlife Sanctuary otherwise devoted to a celebration of romanticized nature gives rise to an assumed fundamental ontological separatism between notionally 'Black' ('Indigenous') and 'White' ('Introduced') Australian identities.

The question of value in tourism emerges in a new perspective on this issue. Indeed, a powerful tension between different concomitant regimes of value can be observed. First, the park and the performers have to manage operational costs. Financial management and accountability hence define an overarching economic regime of value that remains, to a large extent, hidden behind the scenes. The only contact visitors make with the Sanctuary as an economic enterprise is just before the entrance, when they purchase their ticket, and potentially at the very end, when they buy souvenirs or photographic images taken with some of the animals displayed.

Implicitly, this economic regime of value is in tension with the symbolically heightened regime of indigenous nature values that supply the main theme for the displays that visitors encounter. These values are evoked both in the form of an authentic state of animal wilderness whose engagement with Europeans initiates the history of Australian settler society and in the form of a primordial dreamscape residing in contemporary descendants of the Aboriginal and Torres Strait Islands populations. In both cases, indigenous nature defines a value of uncanny otherness – an earlier state of nature that has a sacred ancestry that leads both park visitors and performers back to a presumed lost or hidden quality defining their inner selves.

The two regimes of value are not universally commensurable and different actors apply different rates or logics of conversion. The entry price provides a good example. For the park director, the fee is determined by the logic of economic cost optimization. It must cover the operational costs of the Sanctuary and ideally generate a profit. For some of the indigenous performers, to the contrary, this entry price paid by the visitors is, rhetorically, not regarded as part of the economic regime of value. It is claimed that the specific setting of the indigenous performance unfolds within a sacred realm incommensurable with such a discourse of economic value (as if financial and monetary concerns have a polluting or desacralizing effect).

In responding to this issue of incommensurability, the perspective of the Indigenous performance group positions the entrance fee payment by the visitors as simply accessing a regime of hospitality – the cultural performance is represented in the discourse of the Aboriginal dance troupe as a kind of gift offered by themselves as host both to the non-Indigenous visitors and, as the performers see it, to the hosts' deceased Aboriginal ancestors. In the context of a relatively young post-settler society, Currumbin Wildlife Sanctuary thus addresses a key issue of analysis in the anthropology of tourism, where incommensurable economic and cultural values are so often in tension with production of the plot and play of visitor experiences.

Acknowledgements
We acknowledge collaboration and collegial discussion from Jane Mulcock, Catarina Moreira and Alexis Bunten.

Funding
The collaboration for this project was enabled by support from The University of Queensland (Trigger), University of Southern Queensland (Pocock) and a 2012 University of Queensland Travel Award for International Collaborative Research (Picard). Moreover, part of Picard's research was financed through national funds provided by the Portuguese Foundation for Science and Technology project [PTDC/CS-ANT/114825/2009].

Notes
1. Two species of lorikeet visit Currumbin Wildlife Sanctuary; the dominant species is the Rainbow Lorikeet (*Trichoglossus haematodus*) while smaller numbers of scaly-breasted lorikeets (*Trichoglossus* chlorolepidotus) also appear at feeding times (Barker & Vestjens, 1990, pp. 345–346; Currumbin Wildlife Sanctuary, 2009). Both species are native to this area of northeast Australia.
2. See http://www.cws.org.au/getcloser/visitors_information/faqs/#link14, retrieved January 23, 2014. In a related fashion, it appears that certain koalas are 'selected for handling' at the Lone Pine Koala Sanctuary in Brisbane some 80 km north of Currumbin: http://blog.queensland. com/2013/08/29/cool-jobs-head-koala-keeper/, retrieved January 25, 2014.
3. Though somewhat ironically this can be 'Aboriginal music' actually performed by non-Aboriginal artists, such as Adam Plack (also known as Nomad) who has established an internationally known performance genre focused partly on producing Australian Aboriginal music.

4. For recent discussion of this issue in public debate, see: Pearlman and Gibson (2007), when I was fauna: citizen's rallying call, Sydney Morning Herald, 23 May 2007, http://www.smh.com.au/news/national/when-i-was-fauna-citizens-rallying-call/2007/05/22/1179601412706.html, retrieved January 25, 2014. McQuire (2012), no longer flora and fauna: New South Wales Government commits to heritage legislation, Tracker, 6 November 2012. http://tracker.org.au/2012/11/no-longer-flora-and-fauna-nsw-govt-commits-to-heritage-legislation/, retrieved January 25, 2014.
5. This term may translate as 'brother' in the language of Torres Strait Islands: http://coombs.anu.edu.au/SpecialProj/PNG/MIHALIC/M2/LetterB/bala.htm, retrieved January 25, 2014. It is used more broadly throughout parts of Aboriginal Australia.
6. See http://www.southbank.qm.qld.gov.au/Events+and+Exhibitions/Exhibitions/Permanent/Dandiiri+Maiwar/Ailan+kastom+bilong+Torres+Strait/Dhari#.Uul4uU2IrIU, retrieved January 30, 2014.
7. There was considerable ambiguity in the talk about dingos. They are displayed both within cages as dangerous to humans and yet also walked on leads among the visitors where their role as apex predators is celebrated as beneficial to humans and nature.

References

Barker, R. D., & Vestjens, W. J. M. (1990). *Food of Australian birds*, vol. 1, Non-Passerines. Lyneham, ACT: CSIRO Australia.
Bruner, E. M., & Kirshenblatt-Gimblett, B. (1994). Maasai on the lawn. *Cultural Anthropology, 9*(4), 435–470.
Bunten, A. (2014). Deriding demand: Indigenous imaginaries in tourism. In Noel B. Salazar & Nelson H. H. Graburn (Eds.), *Tourism imaginaries: Anthropological approaches* (pp. 80–102). New York, NY: Berghahn Books.
Currumbin Wildlife Sanctuary. (2009). *Teacher Resources: Lorikeet Arena*. Retrieved January 21, 2014 from http://www.cws.org.au/getcloser/images/pdf/LORIKEET_ARENA-GUIDES_GUIDE.pdf.
Clifford, J. (1989). The others: Beyond the 'salvage' paradigm. *Third Text, 3*(6), 73–78.
DeFrantz, T. F. (2011). Theorizing connectivities: African American women in concert dance. *The Journal of Pan African Studies, 4*(6), 56–74.
Edensor, T. (2000). Staging tourism: Tourists as performers. *Annals of Tourism Research, 27*(2), 322–344.
Goffman, E. (1959). *The presentation of self in everyday life*. New York, NY: Doubleday.
Graburn, N. H. (2013). Anthropology and couchsurfing – variations on a theme. In D. Picard & S. Buchberger (Eds.), *Couchsurfing cosmopolitanisms* (pp. 173–180). Bielefeld: Transcript.
Langton, M. (1996, Summer). What do we mean by wilderness? Wilderness and Terra Nullius in Australian Art. *The Sydney Papers*, 11–31.
Langton, M., & David, B. (2003). William Ricketts Sanctuary, Victoria (Australia) sculpting nature and culture in a primitivist theme park. *Journal of Material Culture, 8*(2), 145–168.
Lash, S., & Urry, J. (1994). *Economies of signs and space*. London: Sage.
MacCannell, D. (1976). *The tourist: A new theory of the leisure class*. Berkeley: University of California Press.
Magowan, F. (2000). Dancing with a difference: Reconfiguring the poetic politics of Aboriginal ritual as national spectacle. *The Australian Journal of Anthropology, 11*(2), 308–321.
McLean, I. (1998). *White aborigines: Identity politics in Australian art*. Cambridge: Cambridge University Press.
McLean, I. (2003). Landscape and ideology: Picturing Sydney Cove 200 years ago. In D. Trigger & G. Griffiths (Eds.), *Disputed territories: Land, culture and identity in settler societies*. Hong Kong (pp. 109–129): Hong Kong University Press.
McQuire, A. (2012). No longer flora and fauna: New South Wales Government commits to heritage legislation. *Tracker Magazine*. Retrieved January 25, 2014, from http://tracker.org.au/2012/11/no-longer-flora-and-fauna-nsw-govt-commits-to-heritage-legislation.
Merlan, F. (1997). Reply to Patrick Wolfe. *Social Analysis, 41*(2), 10–19.
Mulcock, J., & Trigger, D. (2008). Ecology and identity: A comparative perspective on the negotiation of 'nativeness'. In D. Wylie (Ed.), *Toxic belonging? Identity and ecology in southern Africa* (pp. 178–198). Newcastle Upon Tyne: Cambridge Scholars Press.

Nash, D. (1977). Tourism as a form of imperialism. In Valene L. Smith (Ed.), *Hosts and guests: The anthropology of tourism* (pp. 33–47). Philadelphia, PA: University of Pennsylvania Press.

Neuenfeldt, K. (1997). *The didjeridu: From Arnhem Land to the internet.* Sydney: John Libbey Press.

Peace, A. (2001). Dingo discourse: Constructions of nature and contradictions of capital in an Australian eco-tourist location. *Anthropological Forum, 11*, 175–194.

Pearlman, J., & Gibson, J. (2007, May 23). When I was fauna: citizen's rallying call. *The Sydney Morning Herald.* Retrieved January 25, 2014, from http://www.smh.com.au/news/national/when-i-was-fauna-citizens-rallying-call/2007/05/22/1179601412706.html.

Picard, D. (2010). 'Being a model for the world': Performing Creoleness in La Reunion. *Anthropology, 12*(3), 302–315.

Picard, D. (2011). *Tourism, magic and modernity: Cultivating the human garden.* Oxford: Berghahn.

Picard, D. (2012). Tourism, awe and inner journeys. In D. Picard & M. Robinson (Eds.), *Emotion in motion: Tourism, affect and transformation* (pp. 1–20). London: Ashgate.

Picard, D. (2013). What it feels like to be a tourist: Explorations into the meaningful experiences of ordinary mass tourists, Ethnologia Europaea. *Journal of European Ethnology, 43*(1), 5–18.

Picard, D., & Di Giovine, M. (Eds.). (2014). *Tourism and the power of otherness: Seductions of difference.* Bristol: Channel View.

Picard, D., & Zuev, D. (2014). The tourist plot: Antarctica and the modernity of nature. *Annals of Tourism Research, 45*, 102–115.

Robinson, R. S. (2000). *Dreaming tracks: History of the Aboriginal Islander skills development scheme, 1972–1979: Its place in the continuum of Australian indigenous dance and the contribution of its African American founder, Carole Y. Johnson.* Nepean: University of Western Sydney.

Rose, D. B. (1997). The year zero and the North Australian frontier. In D. B. Rose & A. F. Clarke (Eds.), *Tracking knowledge in North Australian landscapes: Studies in Indigenous and settler ecological knowledge systems* (pp. 19–36). Casuarina, NT: Australian National University North Australia Research Unit.

Trigger, D., Mulcock, J., Gaynor, A., & Toussaint, Y. (2008). Ecological restoration, cultural preferences and the symbolic politics of 'nativeness' in Australia. *Geoforum, 39*, 1273–1283.

Waitt, G. (1999). Naturalizing the 'primitive': A critique of marketing Australia's indigenous peoples as 'hunter-gatherers'. *Tourism Geographies, 1*(2), 142–163, viewed January 14, 2014.

Walker, K. (2010). My courageous conversation. In M. Evans (Ed.), *My courageous conversation* (pp. 39–44). Melbourne: University of Melbourne.

White, R. (1981). *Inventing Australia: Images and identity 1688–1980.* Sydney: George Allen & Unwin.

Wolfe, P. (1991). On being woken up: The dreamtime in anthropology and in Australian settler culture. *Comparative Studies in Society and History, 33*(2), 197–224.

Wolfe, P. (1994). Nation and miscegenation: Discursive continuity in the post-Mabo era. *Social Analysis, 36*, 93–152.

Shifting values of 'primitiveness' among the Zafimaniry of Madagascar: an anthropological approach to tourist mediators' discourses

Fabiola Mancinelli

Department of Social and Cultural Anthropology, University of Barcelona, Barcelona, Spain

This article studies the origins, the production and the ambivalent uses of a 'primitive narrative' about the Zafimaniry of Madagascar. The analysis focuses on tourism mediators' discourses and how they are challenged by the actual tourists' experiences; it is based on participant observation, interviews and web analysis. From national tour operators to local tour guides, the mediators' communicative staging of the Zafimaniry recalls and broadens the notion of 'primitiveness', using it as an element of fascination and nostalgia. However, the actual tourists' experience questions this perspective, responding with a 'philanthropic' narrative, a desire to engage in action and relieve from poverty. Both discourses reveal however of a comparative nature and stem from the same logic: a way of 'meeting the Other' from a Western perspective.

As much as tourism is an enormous profit-generating business, it is also an industry that produces, distributes and consumes narratives, imaginaries, identities and, ultimately, dreams. This production is generally shaped according to the consumer identities of tourist-generating countries that are, in their majority and at least so far, affluent European regions.[1] The imaginaries and narratives constructed through and for tourism are powerful: they have the power to move people, but also to travel on a global scale, spreading their system of representations beyond spatial and cultural boundaries. By doing so, they mobilize and create 'regimes of value', in the sense that they confer meaning or importance to a number of things, tangible – such as services or material objects, and intangible – such as social relationships, emotions, exchanges, etc. These become, at the same time, 'desirable' and 'worth': that is 'values', in a sociological and economic sense (Graeber, 2001). Desirable, because, as it has been argued (Ateljevic & Doorne, 2003), in predominantly 'Western' cultures, leisure and tourism consumption are vehicles of social differentiation means for increasing what Bourdieu (1984) defined as 'cultural capital'. 'Worth' because they have an ultimate economic sense, which is measured by 'how much others are willing to give up to get them' (Graeber, 2001).

In times when an ever-greater proportion of the world population can afford to travel, the desire of differentiation leads to the construction of products and experiences ever more heterogeneous, multiplying the labels to give consumers the feeling of belonging to a 'selected crowd'. If tourism is, at least in one of its manifold senses, a form of 'appropriation of otherness' (Harkin, 1995), the value aspect inherent to this acknowledgement goes beyond the strictly economic mechanism of the industry, bringing the social valorization of intangible resources that had not previously been considered for display or sharing. We can see some examples in the popularity of phenomena such as favela tours or war tourism, passing through distinct forms of experiential tourism, to name but a few. In this broader process of valorization, accomplished through and for tourism, an important role is played by the representations of societies and their past (Rassool & Witz, 1996). In fact, tourism is also related to the production and transmission of heritage and historical knowledge, but how this is accomplished depends often on power relations and ideologies. This phenomenon becomes particularly evident in the conceptual framing of experiences of 'the authentic' or 'the exotic', encounters with cultures of distant societies, especially with a colonial past. These constitute privileged sites, where the production of determined forms of value and meaning can be observed and analysed.

This article is an exploration of the origins and the transformations of a 'primitivist narrative' in tourism mediators' discourses around the Zafimaniry, a community of swidden cultivators and woodcarvers living in the mountains of central Madagascar. I want to examine how anthropological terminology travels from ethnography to cultural tourism, contributing to create a value of 'primitiveness' used to market a destination to Western tourists.

The notions of 'primitive' and 'primitiveness' have mainly been analysed in reference to ethnographic arts (Clifford, 1988; Errington, 1998; Myers, 2006; Price, 1989) and are certainly problematic when applied to people and societies (Chabloz, 2009). However, depending on different settings of experience, they can convey a much broader imaginary with manifold meanings. Representations connected with an imaginary of 'primitiveness' and 'traditional society' are increasingly present in cultural tourism, but the use and nuances of this vocabulary within the tourism industry are relatively unexamined (Abbink, 1999, 2000; Chabloz, 2009; Cohen, 1989; Deutschlander & Miller, 2003; Rassool & Witz, 1996). In the perspective I hope to build, the expression 'primitivist narrative' is used in an inclusive way, incorporating a set of representations related to the value of the past, of the 'archaic', of the 'primitive' and the 'tribal'. Although all these expressions do not hold equivalent meaning from a scientific point of view, one can consider them as representations of a specific way of 'meeting the other', of conceiving and defining 'Otherness'. How is the value of the 'primitivist narrative' created and established within our case study? How does it travel and is it redefined through the different languages of ethnography, heritage and tourism? How is it used in tourism narratives?

The analysis presented in this paper is taken from a larger project about processes of commodification, institutional heritage-making and tourism development of the Zafimaniry of Madagascar. Data were drawn from a diversified corpus of resources: participant observation during several visits to the villages over 11 months of fieldwork; conversations and semi-structured interviews with tourism mediators and tourists in the villages; ethnographic literature and website advertising.

Missionaries and ethnographers

The Zafimaniry are a community of about 35,000 people, living in almost 50 villages scattered in a vast area in the mountains of central Madagascar, near the city of Ambositra. Their territory, a set of steep mountains separated by narrow valleys, is enclosed between the central highlands and the eastern escarpment, overlooking an area still covered in rainy forest, also known as 'the corridor'. The Zafimaniry are related to the Merina and the Betsileo (Bloch, 1975; Coulaud, 1973), two major groups inhabiting the Malagasy highlands. In the nineteenth century, they left their original settlement, probably around the capital Antananarivo, fleeing the political unrest resulting from the hegemonic project of a Merina kingdom, and came to settle in the harsh territory they occupy nowadays, humid and uneasy to access. As a result of their emplacement in what once was dense primary forest, they have developed excellent woodwork abilities, visible in the architecture and decoration of their houses. In 2003, their woodcarving knowledge was declared Masterpiece of the Oral and Intangible Heritage of Humanity by the UNESCO and inscribed in 2008 on the Representative List of Cultural Intangible Heritage.

A small-scale movement of visitors in the region, forerunner of what can be considered modern tourism, started back in the late 1960s, after the 'discovery' of their woodcarving art driven by two key factors: the Catholic evangelization movement and the first ethnographic expedition in the area, in 1964. The arrival of the Catholic missionaries had a significant effect on the traditional woodcarving practice of this group: concerned about the lack of revenues of the population, the fathers encouraged a bigger scale production and helped local craftsmen find commercial outlets for their products (Bloch, 1980). Ground was laid for a double dynamic: on the one hand, Zafimaniry traditional products began to circulate beyond the boundaries of the region; on the other, friends and guests of the mission started to venture in this remote region hoping to bring home an 'authentic' Zafimaniry (Coulaud, 1973). The visitors on these first circuits used local populations as guides and stayed at the mission or in private houses (Coulaud, 1973). Following this early curiosity, in 1964, a team of French academic representatives departed to 'the discovery of Zafimaniry culture and its sculptors' (Hammer & Vérin, 2004, p. 13). The ethnographic exhibition-sale that followed the expedition, held in Antananarivo that same year, received much attention: in the 1970s the popularity of Zafimaniry crafts became so huge that an article published in a magazine of the time asked: 'Who doesn't have his own Zafimaniry, yet?' quoted by Coulaud (1973, p. 302). The discourses produced by French ethnologists create a narrative about the Zafimaniry, focused on their woodcarving practice and its relationship with the origins of Madagascar. For the anthropologist Vérin (1964), Zafimaniry villages remind of the capital Antananarivo as it was 130 years before: 'This region has gathered the civilization of the wooded highlands and passed it on to today. It is therefore a true laboratory for the study of Malagasy past' (Vérin, 1972, p. 116). The geographer Daniel Coulaud equally insists upon this aspect, highlighting that: 'the Zafimaniry country represents nowadays a fascinating full-size living museum of the lifestyle, the type of house construction and the art of Malagasy highlands in the past centuries' (Coulaud, 1989, p. 35). Coulaud considers Zafimaniry civilization to be 'archaic' (Coulaud, 1973, p. 90) and 'fossil': 'Thanks to their isolation, the Zafimaniry constitute a fossil group, a society of the past, particularly on the material level' (Coulaud, 1973, p. 109). In this perspective, the Zafimaniry represent the persistence of tradition and a breathing example of the history of Malagasy highlands.

The narrative created by the ethnologists is adopted, a few years later, by the Direction of Cultural Heritage (DCH) of the Malagasy Ministry of Culture, which promotes the labelling of Zafimaniry woodcarving knowledge as Intangible Heritage of Humanity by the UNESCO. In the documents produced for the process, the Zafimaniry are presented as an 'authentic, preserved culture' (UNESCO, 2008). The woodcarving is presented as 'a mean to affirm Zafimaniry cultural identity' (DCH, 2003, p. 18), where the Zafimaniry are defined as: 'the last representatives of a tradition disappeared in Malagasy Highlands' (DCH, 2003, p. 17), their villages as 'open air museums' (2003, p. 3). The language chosen by the technicians of DCH to present the Zafimaniry to the UNESCO creates an image of this people as living in an 'intimate relationship with nature' (2003, p. 4). Great emphasis is placed on their isolation, and on the originality and authenticity of their culture, together with the fear for its imminent disappearance, recalled to justify the need for safeguarding.

I suggest that the master narrative created by ethnologists and adopted by the DCH, with its emphasis upon the 'society of the past', introduces the Zafimaniry into a 'regime of value' (Appadurai, 1986). This regime is culturally constructed through the 'gaze of the Other' and is based on what can be called a poetics of time, established on the construction of the past as something made valuable and meaningful over the present. This statement stands as a 'taxonomic moment' (Clifford, 1988), as the notion of the past as something to be preserved is a social construction, a value for societies particularly conscious of their history and Western ones in particular. It is through a Western classificatory system that the old – conceptualized in different ways that may include the traditional, the primitive, the authentic – is erected as a value that transcends time. So framed, the value of the Zafimaniry, established through the language of Western ethnography and ratified by an international labelling, quickly becomes transcendent of cultural boundaries and part of a 'global taxonomic system' (Palumbo, 2011) or a 'global hierarchy of value' (Herzfeld, 2004). As one key feature of the 'primitivist narrative', this poetics of time is structured around two central axes, such that we can trace in both the ethnographic and heritage discourse: the 'denial of coevalness' (Fabian, 1983) and the idea of 'vanishing culture'. The 'denial of coevalness' consists in considering that 'other' people, non-Western or 'traditional' societies are timeless, and located in a time outside history (Errington, 1998; Fabian, 1983), an eternal present that does not change. This recognition is intertwined to the second of our conceptual axes: the idea of 'vanishing culture' implicitly acting in conservation and heritage ideologies. With reference to heritage-making processes, Bortolotto (2008) notes that the idea of 'endangered culture' is clearly tendentious, as it implicitly considers that there is a pre-existing essence to be defended, something original that should not be lost. For the law of equilibrium, if non-Western societies are always presented on the edge of modernization and disappearance, the task of the Western world is to rescue them and safeguard them, as 'ethnographic' cultures, primitive 'arts' (Clifford, 1998, p. 235) or heritage. How is this cultural framework appropriated and transformed through tourism in reference to the Zafimaniry? How does the imaginary of a 'society of the past', shaped by ethnographic accounts, travel and is converted into a value within the tourism discourse?

The Zafimaniry as a tourist attraction

I will now examine the transformative trajectory through which the narrative of the Zafimaniry as 'living past' re-emerges and circulates through the discourses of tourism mediators, in the form of 'communicative staging' (Cohen, 1989). The international touristic image of Madagascar is built around its extraordinary ecological biodiversity in flora and fauna, 80% of which is endemic. Despite this exceptional endowment, it is one of the poorest countries in the world (Human Development Index, 2013 [http://hdr.undp.org/sites/default/files/Country-Profiles/MDG.pdf]). Tourism, with the niche of the ecotourism market, has long been considered a key element in the country's development strategy (Sarrasin, 2007). Beside the coasts and the sea, the main attraction for tourists travelling to Madagascar is its natural parks – six of which are listed as UNESCO World Heritage sites – and the observation of local wildlife, particularly lemurs (Sarrasin, 2007). However, severe environmental degradation is leading to the capitalization of other elements, such as cultural heritage, traditions and beliefs, as other reasons to discover the country. The 2012 promotional campaign of the Madagascar National Tourism Board extends the invitation to 'travel through time' and 'discover the Malagasy people', 'far beyond their legendary smile' (http://www.madagascar-tourisme.com/en).

Paralleling this capitalization of cultural assets, the fame of the Zafimaniry has increased over the years. The circuit of informal tourism mentioned in the previous paragraph has turned into something more structured and the Zafimaniry are becoming one of the 'tourist attractions' of the RN7, the famous national road connecting the capital Antananarivo to the south of the country.[2] The destination cannot yet be considered a very developed tourist situation,[3] although this may probably change very soon.

The gate to the region is the village of Antoetra. With its 2000 inhabitants, it conserves very little resemblance with the rest of Zafimaniry villages. However, as it can be easily reached in one hour by car from Ambositra, for guides and tourists short of time the village has become 'the capital of the Zafimaniry'. Older and smaller Zafimaniry villages can only be reached on foot, through a dense network of very narrow paths that clamber up the mountains. Trekking through this area is an increasingly popular option for people passionate for mountain hiking, interested in nature and landscape, as well as cultural tourism. They either come for the day or choose to overnight in the area. The great majority are French or Italian nationals: couples in their honeymoon or retired people. They have travelled to other 'exotic' destinations and are inclined to connect with 'real people'. Their motivations are not related as much, as it was in the 1970s, to the commodification of Zafimaniry crafts: the Zafimaniry themselves, with their culture and traditional lifestyle, have become the tourist attraction.

The European tour operator

All the most popular travel guidebooks about Madagascar – Lonely Planet, Routard, Petit Futé – increasingly make mention of the Zafimaniry region and of the UNESCO's recognition to the woodcarving. Similarly, a number of International Tour Operators propose a circuit in this region as part of their offer. In the opinion of one of them, the creation of the Zafimaniry as a 'tourist destination' owes as much to Tour Operators suggestions than to tourists' interests: very few people know or have expectations about the Zafimaniry beforehand; they find out once touring Madagascar. It seems therefore appropriate to analyse how an experience among the Zafimaniry is framed in the language of touristic advertising, in order to understand how tourists' expectations are set.

The most significant examples for my analysis are two popular Antananarivo-based tour operators, both owned by Europeans. To market an excursion to the Zafimaniry villages through their websites, they choose a language that reproduces different kinds of the concept of 'living past'. On the website of one of them, the visit to the Zafimaniry is described as 'a step back hundred years in the past, into an endearing and fascinating medieval world' [http://www.papavelotrekking.com/randonnee-zafimaniry-grand-tour-nord-ou-grand-tour-sud.php (Retrieved May 20, 2010)]. The same register is also adopted by the bestselling agency in the area, whose website defines the Zafimaniry as: 'one of the last animist tribes of Madagascar'. On an issue of the corporative review of the agency, they are referred to as the 'lost tribe' [http://www.fronterasdepapel.com/enero2009/pais_zafimaniry_info.htm (Retrieved May 7, 2013)]. Guillaume,[4] the owner of the agency, is very well known within the local community: European, a former journalist and anthropologist by education, he has been bringing tourists in the area for over a decade. He discovered the Zafimaniry during one journalistic trip to Madagascar, loved the region and decided to create a small tour operator to promote it. In a way, Guillaume can be considered as one of the drivers of modern tourism in the area. When asked to explain his presentation of the Zafimaniry, he pointed out that:

> [The Zafimaniry] are guarantors of a culture and lifestyle that are disappearing in Madagascar. For me, they are the last pure ones, the last survivors of those first migrations of Merina and Betsileo that arrived on the island 1200 years ago. (…)Their *modus vivendi* responds to the model that in Africa would be called 'tribal': autonomy, independence of the villages for many things, little contact with modern medicine. In Madagascar we are afraid to use the word *tribe*, while in Africa it is used much more easily. (Personal communication, August 2012)

The conceptualization of the Zafimaniry as 'the last pure ones' is consistent with the discourse established by ethnography, and reproduces the idea of 'vanishing culture', as my interlocutor defines the Zafimaniry as 'one of the last living examples of the pre-modern lifestyle of the first inhabitants of the island'. This 'primitivist narrative', to which the tour operator makes explicit reference, is however broadened by the introduction of the term 'tribe'. To justify it, Guillaume discusses their cultural integrity: Zafimaniry 'animist' religious beliefs, and a culture dominated by orality. He also commented on their resistance to change, somehow ambiguously threatened by their growing touristic popularity, 'prostituting their culture' as he said:

> I do not want the villages to prostitute themselves in a very touristic way, as it's already happened to some of them. I don't want the more interior villages to change: they never asked to change. There are many villages that are good the way they are, living as they live, and nobody asked us to do anything, they do not want to progress. (Personal communication, August 2012)

Guillaume's framing of the Zafimaniry shows us an example of the use of a 'primitivist narrative'. The choice of the term 'tribe', as much as the notion of 'primitive' or 'traditional society', belongs to the logic of representation shared by the evolutionist and anthropological theories of the eighteenth and nineteenth century. For the evolutionists, 'primitive societies' represents an earlier stage on the development of 'civilized ones'. Anthropology found its object on the understanding and analysis of these original states of humanity, supported by the belief that 'progress' and 'civilization' were to be a common destiny. In the anthropological theories of the nineteenth century, the term 'tribe' was used as 'a convenient initial descriptive label' (Southall, 1970) to describe culturally unitary groups, linguistic, cultural, ideological and structural entities (Radcliffe-Brown as cited in Berndt, 1959), sharing a particular way of life. However, at a closer examination, it can be argued that there is certain vagueness when it comes to its empirical substance (Berndt, 1959, p. 81); the word 'tribe' defines alterity by negation: it indicates something less complex, less advanced or less rational. From a scientific point of view, the use of terms such as 'traditional society', 'tribe' and 'primitive' have long revealed their descriptive inadequacy (Southall, 1970): they are not based on objective ontological features of a given society, but rather result from a form of comparative judgement that opposes, to a series of characteristics established as indicators of civilization by Western thought, their absence. They can thus be considered dialogical social constructions (Clifford, 1988; Errington, 1998; Mudimbe, 1988; Myers, 2006; Price, 1989), historically determined classifying devices embedded in a power–knowledge relationship between a dominant, hegemonic culture and an object alien to it (Mudimbe, 1988). However, the point I want to make is that, in their transition from social science to tourism, they become functional to the creation of an 'exotic', 'authentic' image of a destination. As Bruner and Kirshenblatt-Gimblett (1994, p. 435) note: 'Tourism gives tribalism and colonialism a second life by bringing them back as representations of themselves and circulating them within an economy of performance.'

The fascination of 'the primitive'

In both its use by nineteenth-century anthropologists and the tour operators' discourse, the 'primitivist narrative' transmitted by the word 'tribe' evokes an epistemological distinction between Europe and what is outside. However, I suggest that there is a significant shift, as in tourism 'the primitive' comes to hold the characteristics of something ambiguously fascinating, an alterity that can be glanced at and experienced through the relatively comfortable and safe setting created by mediators. Clearly, the choice of this framing is an invitation to the tourists' quest for authenticity and social differentiation. In an industry that sells imaginaries and dreams, desire for alterity and ephemeral – and in most cases controlled – getaways, the notion of 'tribe' comes to embody the possibility of a 'search of lost time', a pre-colonial past and an alternative lifestyle in the rapidly homogenizing world where the tourists come from. A world that makes visitors sigh for its simplicity, as if it were something really closer to the origins.

This 'primitivist narrative' responds to the increasing fascination that tourism-generating countries show for 'lost' or 'endangered' traditions and lifestyles. We can consider it as part of a much broader process, that is, the incorporation of the 'primitive' in the global economy (Errington, 1998). The tourism sector is a domain where this fascination for 'the primitive' emerges strongly, through experiences classified as 'ethnic' or 'mystical' tourism. But it can be traced also in the artistic domain, with the emergence of 'world culture', or in new food trends, reintroducing the cereals of our ancestors[5] (Amselle, 2010), as well as in cultural and heritage polities.

One may consider this fascination a form of nostalgia. Graburn (1995) notes how nostalgia, the sentimental longing for feelings and things of the past, is one of the most powerful forces for tourist attraction. Rosaldo (1989) names a special version of it, when he refers to 'imperialist nostalgia', a regret that people of the Western World have for 'traditional culture', 'the very culture that the colonialists have intentionally altered or destroyed' (Bruner, 1989, p. 108). It is the nostalgia for 'the good that is old', the charming power of what in Western societies, through the expansion of capitalism and the massification of globalization, has been lost forever (cf. Amselle, 2010). 'It is precisely this traditional culture that the tourists come to see (...). Tourists long for the pastoral, for their origins, for the unpolluted, the pure, and the original' (Bruner, 1989, p. 439). However, this fascination and its correlate of nostalgia remain largely ethnocentric, as reflections of a hierarchy, of knowledge and power. It results from decisions taken within established 'regimes of value', about what deserves to be preserved and what, on the other hand, should be lost. It is an impulse that justifies the conservation of a 'vanishing culture', but also stirs up their 'museification':

One might object that the glorification of the traditional is the one reliable means of ensuring its preservation; and indeed it is so. But that act of preservation is a dramatic example of the musei-fication of living populations that Johannes Fabian has identified as the mark of survivalism in anthropological discourse but that is in fact a pervasive feature of high modernism in general. (Herzfeld, 2004, p. 31)

Local tour guides and tourists

At a different level of the commercialization of the Zafimaniry destination, the discourse of Malagasy tour guides and the tourists' reactions must also be looked at. Here, 'the primi-tivist narrative' is proposed again, but yet another small turn is given to its meaning. For tourists who do not travel with organized groups, the encounter with the Zafimaniry is pre-pared in Ambositra, with the meeting of local tour guides working for small tour operators. They are all Malagasy, work independently and in competition with one another. According to one local tour guide from Ambositra:

[An excursion in the Zafimaniry villages] is a great opportunity to see how people lived in the past, in a primitive village. (…) It is a very interesting place to visit, with its beautiful wooden houses and breath-taking views. However, it is not an excursion that suits everybody. You know, not many tourists dare to spend a night in the villages: the Zafimaniry are very poor and dirty, Western tourists are not always at ease (…). (Personal communication, October 2008)

In this discourse, that echoes similar versions heard in Ambositra, it is the first time that the word 'primitive' is openly used. The particular context caught my attention because I found it significantly ambivalent, playing with the fascination of the 'primitive' as well as with the reference to 'dirtiness' and 'poverty'. On the one hand, the guide presented the cultural elements that would make an excursion to the Zafimaniry 'desirable': traditional beliefs, a lifestyle in close contact with nature, the mysterious origins of their woodcarving skills and the beauty of their architecture. In this first meaning, he was using the term 'primitive' in an assertive, positive way, referring to something unique, somehow closer to the origins. On the other hand, he immediately challenged this expectation referring to the 'cultural remoteness' of this people, recalling the 'poor' living conditions and the 'dirtiness' of the population. He stressed their geographic isolation, the hardships of the path to get there, and the shortage of food and comfort. Food safety was especially stressed upon, prob-ably anticipating the tourists' primary concern for the hygienic conditions and the fear to get sick. All these elements were used to justify the need for guiding, protection and basic services that he was offering. This guide was proposing himself as a 'native interpreter of the culture' (McKean, 1976), a local broker mediating between two entirely different worlds. In doing so, however, he provided an image of reality interpreted through Western standards, making local culture appear like something distant and mysterious. Adopting this strategy of 'localization' (Salazar, 2005), he deliberately constructed a narra-tive that 'folklorize, ethnicize and exotize' the Zafimaniry, enhancing the most distant fea-tures from the culture of the interlocutor.

How is this narrative experienced by the tourists? Their visits to the villages share a sort of common pattern: they generally arrive in the villages a couple of hours before sunset, after a long and tiring walk. They are lodged in private houses, whose owners receive a small fee. The villages have no electricity and offer hardly any facilities: one or two latrines in very basic bamboo huts, bucket shower, a small shop that sells beers and refreshments. All provisions are brought from Ambositra. Depending on the guide knowledge and willingness to share, they take a walk around and visit one or two traditional houses, followed by an explanation about the woodcarvings. After, they are left free to roam and take pictures. They mostly come in contact with the youngsters, while the adults remain engaged in their ordinary activities. Children follow visitors closely, with a mixture of curiosity and reverence and expecting to receive some kind of small gifts: t-shirts, pens, candies and used plastic bottles. Sometimes, they ask for money. There is no kind of substantial staging of Zafimaniry identity, nor particular performances; in a way, nothing 'happens'. If there is any daily activity that goes on – such as grinding rice or shelling beans – and tourists show the will to participate, they are invited to get involved. When the sun sets, visitors retire in the house where they are lodged and eat their food in company of their guide and porters. In some cases, the guides may make some music and indulge in drinking local rum and beers. When this happens, some young male villagers join in. In the morning, the tourists pay a visit to the chief of the village, where they share a toast of the local rum (*toaka gasy*) and receive a blessing. This ritual moment is an occasion of mutual thanksgiving, during which the local guide instructs the tourists to leave a small gift of money.

According to tourists' discourses, they felt 'welcome' and sometimes felt that they themselves were 'the attraction'. They were impressed by the 'authenticity' of the encounter and amazed by the 'simplicity' of the people. In many cases, they made commentaries about their 'poor' living conditions: their clothes 'dirty and torn' and the 'high number of children'. Two French ladies in their 40s, on a two day trek, commented:

> We were transported into a different world, in the past. We were more surprised by their poverty than by the beauty of the architecture. We had already visited poor countries. We have been in Mali. But here: how they live! 16 in a household, there must be incest all the time. Such promiscuity!

Driven by the images of a 'preserved culture', when they arrive in the villages, tourists seemed most of all confronted and 'touched' by poverty. If the initial goal of the trip was to encounter local people, admire the beauty of their architecture and get to know their lifestyle, the contact with the actual living conditions of the Zafimaniry brings about a whole set of preconceived images regarding 'progress' and 'development'. Observation has proved that this confrontation engages, in almost all cases, a philanthropic attitude,[6] a desire to 'do something', most of the time translated into a money donation to the chief of the village, requesting him to buy something useful for the whole community. The desire to help is ambiguously manipulated by local guides who often use it to their own benefit. A couple of young Italian tourists, after a two day visit in the villages, decided to buy a weeder to help the villagers work their rice fields. They went to the market to buy it and left the guide the responsibility to deliver it, which he did not do: he shared the money with the vendor instead. Due to their ephemeral stay in the villages and the language barrier, tourists rarely establish a significant relationship with their hosts. According to some guides, the confrontation with what they consider 'extreme poverty' makes them uneasy and willing to go. A tour guide commented that: 'Tourists do not enjoy being with poor people. Their condition makes them sad' (personal communication, August 2008).

The philanthropic attitude acts in the discourses of tourism mediators as well: very often, tourism professionals have been heard conceptualizing their profit-making business as a beneficial endeavour for the local population. Guillaume, the European tour operator I mentioned before, said: 'We give to the villagers a series of materials to which they normally do not have access: blankets, sugar, salt. And every time we send a group to overnight, we send some small gifts.' In other cases, local tour guides from Ambositra high-lighted their direct implication in the welfare of the community, spending a great deal of time illustrating a number of development projects they intended to carry on in the villages. For example, Frankie, a guide from Ambositra, talked to me about his idea to finance a com-munity association with his tip money, while Dinah, his colleague, mentioned his project for a nursery to fight deforestation. It seems less interesting to investigate whether or how these projects were put in place than to inquire into the necessity of my interlocutors to talk about them. They were expressing their goodwill to return something to the Zafimaniry, as if they were morally obliged to offer compensation for the profit they were making or to justify tourism as a form of social engagement. At the same time, this narrative implies a sort of evaluation, of Zafimaniry and rural communities, as it implies a dichotomy between 'us' and 'them', where 'us', the collective subject including the guide, represents the city, for many a synonym of modernity and development, while 'them' is the countryside, meaning backwardness, poverty and lack of education. This discursive distancing is embedded in a paternalistic background, depicting the Zafimaniry as 'people in need', of support and guidance. Moreover, this aspect of the philanthropic attitude revealed the inter-iorization of a *modus operandi* shaped on the conduct of international NGO's, mostly Western. The emerging value of the 'primitive' as an element of the touristic experience is subtly transformed into an instrument to awake tourists' consciousness and their experi-ence is communicatively framed as a way to relieve people of poverty and to promote the development of a community.

The emergence of a philanthropic attitude in the mediators' discourses and in tourists' intentions is suggestive because it appears within the 'primitivist narrative' itself and can be regarded as the other side of it, arising when an imaginary becomes embodied into a lived experience. The experience of a 'medieval world' that, to quote a tour operator's advertising, is both 'fascinating' and 'endearing' [http://www.papavelotrekking.com/randonnee-zafima niry-grand-tour-nord-ou-grand-tour-sud.php (Retrieved May 20, 2010)]. By opening up the possibility of a philanthropic repercussion, the voyeurism implicit in the tourists' gaze is neutralized and its object is converted into something that is not passively gazed upon, but can be, to a certain extent, interacted with, through a sort of engagement. If the value of the 'primitive' is a reason to motivate tourists to visit the Zafimaniry, 'poverty' is the 'endearing' element: it is part of the picture, one more element of 'exoticization'. In this context, philanthropy seems to stem from the same logic of the 'primitivist narrative', as a part of it, a specific way of 'meeting the Other'. Despite all this, however, this discourse does not escape what Edward Bruner calls 'the trapping power of a paradoxical predicament' (1995, p. 225) because as much as tourists' mediators seem to encourage tourism as a path to economic development, they are aware that the 'more primitive' the people, the more interest they will have for Occidental tourists.

Conclusions

The case study of the Zafimaniry allows us to make some considerations about the use and the shifting meanings of a 'primitivist' narrative within the tourism discourse, and how it is embedded into a 'regime of value'.

In times of growing mass tourism, the language of tourism responds to the need of increasing social differentiation demanded by consumers. This need leads to the valoriza-tion of elements that before were not considered as commodities. These reclassifications not only redefine the status of the objects and experiences taken into consideration, but may also imply subtle shifts in their meaning. In the case study I have analysed, the transition of anthropological terminology to the communicative staging of cultural tourism results in the construction of a 'primitivist narrative' that is significantly ambivalent. When it is evoked, it does not recall only the set of information normally associated to it – such as, for example, the lack of development and technological sophistication, the belief in magical forces or a certain violence in social relations– but also their positive and charming version, a dream of alternative lifestyles, authenticity and unspoilt traditions, depicting images of lost harmonies and life in contact with nature. This 'primitivist narrative' acquires its charming power because, if compared with the worlds where the tourists come from, it gives them the possibility to experience a supposedly radical alterity, the possibility of tra-velling back to the past, following a form of nostalgia that authors have highlighted as one of the most powerful forces of tourist attraction. Tourism offers then the possibility to dom-esticate this 'primitiveness' and experience it from the safe and controlled point of view of a mediated perspective.

However, the actual experiences tourists have at the destination challenge the commu-nicative framing focused on the fascination of the 'primitive'. In our case study, the ambi-guity of experiencing a 'traditional', 'primitive' lifestyle from a wealthy yet concerned Western perspective leads to the emergence of a counter-narrative: a 'philanthropic' one, consisting in the expressed desires of tourists to help the community to improve their poor living conditions. The mutual rapport between the 'primitivist' and the 'philanthropic' narrative makes us think that a form of social engagement can be considered a way to neu-tralize the voyeurism implicit in the tourist gaze and open up to the interpretation of forms of 'ethical tourism' as socially responsible activities, sometimes regardless of their actual practical outcomes. Both these narratives stem from the same logic and are one part of the other: two mutually intertwined ways of 'meeting the Other' from a Western perspective.

Acknowledgements

The author would like to thank the editors and the reviewers for their helpful suggestions and comments.

Funding

The research for this article was partially financed by a FI grant for the training of Research Personnel issued by the Government of Catalonia [grant number FI-DGR 2008–2010].

Notes

1. According to the global ranking of tourism-generating regions, Europe is currently the top source market for tourists, generating 55% of all international tourists, followed by Asia and the Pacific (20%) and the Americas (16%). The explosive growth of the Chinese travel industry has pushed it into the top five even though its population has only just begun to travel. The ranking is expressed in terms of international tourism expenditures. Source: www.wto.com.
2. There is currently an important ecotourism development plan interesting the Zafimaniry region, financed by the European agency A.C.O.R.D.S. [http://www.tourisme.gov.mg/?p=1276. Con-sulted on 18/05/2013].
3. According to the information provided by the local town hall, the villages receive about 2500 visits per year (2008). Numbers have doubled from 2000 to 2008.
4. All names provided in the articles have been changed.
5. The increasing popularity of cereals such as the buckwheat, grown by Ancient Romans, or the amaranth of the Incas or the quinoa, cultivated by native of Andean Highlands can be good examples of this tendency.

6.   The small NGO Babakoto, run by a French couple and active for over 10 years in the region, started from a tourist encounter.

References

Abbink, J. (1999). The production of 'primitiveness' and identity. Surma-tourists interactions. In R. Fardon, R. A. van Dijk, & W. M. J. van Binsbergen (Eds.), *Modernity on a shoestring: Dimensions of globalization, consumption and development in Africa and beyond* (pp. 341–358). Leiden: Eidos.

Abbink, J. (2000). Tourism and its discontents. Suri-tourists encounters in southern Ethiopia. *Social Anthropology, 8*(1), 1–17.

Amselle, J. L. (2010). *Rétrovolutions: Essais sur les primitivismes contemporains.* Paris: Stock Hachette.

Appadurai, A. (1986). Introduction: Commodities and the politics of value. In A. Appadurai (Ed.), *The social life of things* (pp. 3–63). Cambridge: Cambridge University Press.

Ateljevic, I., & Doorne, S. (2003). Culture, economy and tourism commodities: Social relations for production and consumption. *Tourist Studies, 3*(2), 123–141.

Berndt, R. (1959). The concept of "the tribe" in the Western Desert of Australia. *Oceania, 30*(2), 81–107.

Bloch, M. (1975). Property and the end of affinity. In M. Bloch (Ed.), *Marxist analyses in social anthropology* (pp. 203–228). London: Malaby.

Bloch, M. (1980). Modes of production and slavery in Madagascar: Two case studies. In J. L. Watson (Ed.), *Asian and African systems of slavery* (pp. 100–133). Berkeley, CA: University of California Press.

Bortolotto, C. (2008). *Il patrimonio immateriale secondo l'UNESCO: analisi e prospettive.* Milano: Hoepli.

Bourdieu, P. (1984). *Distinction.* London: Routledge.

Bruner, E. (1989). Of cannibals, tourists, and ethnographers. *Cultural Anthropology, 4*(4), 438–445. Blackwell.

Bruner, E. (1995). The ethnographer/tourist in Indonesia. In M. F. Lanfant, J. Allcock, & E. Bruner (Eds.), *International tourism: Identity and change* (pp. 224–241). London: Sage.

Bruner, E., & Kirshenblatt-Gimblett, B. (1994). Maasai on the lawn. Tourist realism in East Africa. *Cultural Anthropology, 9*, 435–470.

Chabloz, N. (2009). *Tourisme et Primitivisme. Cahiers d'études africaines* (Vols. 193–194, pp. 391–428). Paris: EHESS.

Clifford, J. (1988). *The predicament of culture: Twentieth century ethnography, literature and art.* Cambridge, MA: Harvard University Press.

Cohen, E. (1989). 'Primitive and remote'. Hill tribe trekking in Thailand. *Annals of Tourism Research, 16*, 30–61.

Coulaud, D. (1973). *Les Zafimaniry: un groupe ethnique de Madagascar à la poursuite de la forêt.* Antananarivo: Fanotamboky Malagasy.

Coulaud, D. (1989). Arts de la vie et de la survie. *Madagascar, Cahier de l'ADE,* 31–38.

Deutschlander, S., & Miller, L. J. (2003). Politicizing aboriginal cultural tourism: The discourse of primitivism in the tourist encounter. *Canadian Review of Sociology/Revue canadienne de sociologie, 40*(1), 27–44.

Direction of Cultural Heritage (DCH). (2003). *Le savoir-faire du travail du bois dans le pays Zafimaniry, Dossier de Candidature,* Application file for the second proclamation of masterpieces of the oral and intangible heritage of humanity, Ministry of Culture of Madagascar, Antananarivo.

Errington, S. (1998). *The death of primitive art and other tales of progress.* Berkeley, CA: University of California Press.

Fabian, J. (1983). *Time and the other: How anthropology makes its object.* New York: Columbia University Press.

Graburn, N. (1995). Tourism, modernity and Nostalgia. In A. Akbar & C. Shore (Eds.), *The future of anthropology. Its relevance to the contemporary world* (pp. 158–178). Athlone: London & Atlantic Highlands.

Graeber, D. (2001). *Toward an anthropological theory of value: The false coin of our dreams.* Basingstoke: Palgrave MacMillian.

Hammer, J. P., & Vérin, P. (2004). *À Madagascar, chez les Zafimaniry.* Paris: Ibis Press.

Harkin, M. (1995). Modernist anthropology and tourism of the authentic. *Annals of Tourism Research, 22*(3), 650–670.

Herzfeld, M. (2004). *The body impolitic: Artisans and artifice in the global hierarchy of value.* Chicago: University of Chicago Press.

McKean, P. F. (1976, December 8–10). *An anthropological analysis of the culture brokers of Bali: Guides, tourists and Balinese.* Joint UNESCO/IBDR Seminar on the Social and Cultural Impact of Tourism, Washington.

Mudimbe, V. (1988). *The invention of Africa: Gnosis, philosophy, and the order of knowledge.* Bloomington: Indiana University Press.

Myers, F. (2006). Primitivism, anthropology and the category of 'primitive art'. In C. Tilley, S. Kuechler, M. Rowlands, W. Keane, & P. Spyer (Eds.), *Handbook of material culture* (pp. 267–284). London: Sage.

Palumbo, B. (2011). Le alterne fortune di un immaginario patrimoniale. *Antropologia Museale, 28–29,* 8–23.

Price, S. (1989). *Primitive art in civilized places.* Chicago: University of Chicago Press.

Rassool, C., & Witz, L. (1996). South Africa: A world in one country. Moments in international tourist encounters with wildlife, the primitive and the modern. *Cahiers d'études africaines, 36*(143), 335–371.

Rosaldo, R. (1989). *Culture and truth: The remaking of social analysis.* Boston, MA: Beacon Press.

Salazar, N. (2005). Tourism and glocalization: 'Local' tour guiding. *Annals of Tourism Research, 32,* 628–646.

Sarrasin, B. (2007). Géopolitique du tourisme à Madagascar: de la protection de l'environnement au développement de l'économie. *Hérodote, 127*(4), 124–150.

Southall, A. (1970). The Illusion of Tribe. *Journal of African and Asian Studies, 5*(1–2), 28–50.

UNESCO. (2008). *Zafimaniry, une culture conservée. Ny Zafimaniry, nikay ny kolontsainy. Plan d'action de sauvegarde du savoir-faire du travail du bois des Zafimaniry.* Antananarivo, Ministère de la jeunesse, des sports et de la culture.

Vérin, P. (1964). Les Zafimaniry et leur art. Un groupe forestier continuateur d'une tradition esthétique malgache méconnue. *Revue de Madagascar, 27,* 37–48.

Vérin, P. (1972). Notes et comptes rendus: Les Zafimaniry par Daniel Coulaud. *Madagascar, revue de géographie,* 115–118.

Branding Copán: valuing cultural distinction in an archaeological tourism destination

Lena Mortensen

Department of Anthropology, University of Toronto Scarborough, Toronto, Canada

In this article I explore the phenomenon of heritage tourism branding in the country of Honduras, focusing on the archaeological site of Copán, the country's highest profile cultural destination. Branding operates as a primary mode through which tourism value is presumed to circulate and reproduce, and become available for exclusionary regimes to capture new economic rents. As a heightened mechanism for mobilizing symbolic distinction, branding now also appears to organize value well beyond the domain of economic exchange. Branding the past takes on particular resonance in Honduras, where a claim on the ancient Maya, materialized through the Copán Archaeological Park, sustains a significant sector of the tourism market upon which a regional economy now depends. As in other areas of place-based and culture-based tourism, branding practices and logics increasingly dominate the organization of tourism encounters at Copán in both explicit and implicit ways. I use the Honduran case to focus discussion on the many different dimensions of branding that inhere in heritage sites, and the consequences for how such complexes of value are negotiated beyond the market.

Nearly 30 years ago, in a book of the same title, Lowenthal elaborated the idea that the 'past is a foreign country' and, more specifically, 'the foreign country with the healthiest tourist trade of all' (1986, p. 4). Today, the substance of Lowenthal's analysis holds strong: the business of touring the past has moved to encompass nearly every historical period and spatial corner, and heritage tourism is at an all-time high in popularity. The past in this sense functions as a generic reference to destinations framed in temporal terms, and, as destinations, the market value of such places continues to expand (Dallen & Boyd, 2006). Part of what makes this market sector so economically productive is the potent combination of *other* forms of value (e.g. symbolic, aesthetic, atmospheric, emotional) expressed through destinations based around heritage, historic, and archaeological qualities, resulting in something of an enchanted mix that occupies the attention of heritage managers, marketing professionals, and community developers alike (Smith, Messenger, & Soderland, 2010). The functional work of negotiating such incongruent value bundles, often realized through exchanges that rely on distinct but overlapping regimes of evaluation (Appadurai, 1994), raises questions concerning how value itself is calculated, mobilized, and transformed through tourism and its extensions in wider social fields.

Increasingly, the complex mix of value that characterizes heritage tourism contexts is channeled through the work of branding. In cultural tourism, branding is now a common marketing strategy that builds on traditional forms of creating distinction and signaling the unique features that make a destination attractive to potential visitors (Cai, Gartner, & Munar, 2009). As in other commercial sectors, tourism industry operators perceive branding as a predominant mode through which the economic value of tourism circulates, reproduces, and becomes available for exclusionary regimes to capture new rents. However, as I argue below, branding also appears to organize value well beyond the domain of economic exchange. As heritage tourism contexts come to be infused by the logic of branding along different dimensions, they offer a productive angle from which to approach and better understand the dynamics of value in tourism more generally.

Here, I explore the phenomenon of heritage tourism branding in the country of Honduras, focusing specifically on the case of archaeological tourism. Branding the past takes on particular resonance in this small Central American state, where a claim to ancient Maya heritage (a cultural form which, to some extent, itself operates like a brand) sustains a lucrative sector of the tourism market upon which much of the regional economy now relies. I narrow in on the ways in which branding now seems to dominate the organization of tourism encounters at the site of Copán, an archaeological park in western Honduras renowned for its identity as a capital city of the ancient Maya.[1] Though it has undeniable value as a site of archaeological significance, Copán's development as a modern destination has also been guided by forces associated with tourism since at least the 1930s (Mortensen, 2009a). Building on its status as the only UNESCO cultural World Heritage Site within its borders, the government of Honduras promotes Copán as the country's premier attraction for archaeological and heritage tourism in order to generate revenue, for its symbolic value to mark distinction on a global stage, as well as to celebrate an essentialized national identity on the home front (cf. Askew, 2010). These modes of value, though often treated as analytically separate, are intimately linked, even co-constitutive in the making of places into destinations.

The interdependency of symbolic and economic value has become increasingly apparent in recent years as governments, development agencies, marketing professionals, and others assess and seek to capitalize upon the value of culture in concrete terms (Comaroff & Comaroff, 2009; Yudice, 2003). Such approaches to value in effect work to extract economic rents from the domain of the symbolic by operationalizing cultural difference as an entity which can be traded upon, if not traded directly (Harvey, 2002). In cultural tourism, this conjunction of value typically manifests in the transactional exchange of money for culture-based performances and experiences, foods, access to protected areas, heritage sites and other places of display, and for all associated services that facilitate visiting place-based destinations. In this model value is located, or 'added', by means of mapping out distinction or difference amidst a competitive field of alternate tourism opportunities, whether that difference is framed in terms of qualities of place, product, performance, or, in its most complex basis, ethnic identity itself. It is now clear that mobilizing culture for the market on the basis of difference involves much more than quantitative economic reasoning; it extends into complex politics that concern the regulation and control of culturally based expressions, populations, and even bodies, where 'culture', the already-added-value, is presumed to inhere (Anderson, 2013; Scher, 2011).

Branding and value

Recent work in anthropological theory has seen a resurgence in the study of value that focuses on dynamic approaches to how value is created, negotiated, and translated across varied domains and through complex acts of exchange (Eiss & Pedersen, 2002; Graeber, 2001; Miller, 2008). I draw on a conceptual synthesis of this work offered by Ferry (2013), in which value is understood as both the production or 'making' of 'meaningful difference' and, perhaps more usefully, the work of making 'difference meaningful'. In her formulation, 'value-making' is the very process that 'creates and organizes difference', realized over time through a wide range of actions and transactions (Ferry, 2013, p. 11). This approach rests on a concept of value 'as a constellation of action that produces things and qualities, not as a static thing or quality in itself' (Ferry, 2013, p. 20). One critical dimension of 'a constellation of action' that results in value-making is branding, an 'institutionalized method of practically materializing the political economy of signs' (Goldman & Papson, 2006, p. 328). Though precise definition of 'what a brand is or does' remains elusive (Manning, 2010, p. 34), most scholars agree that 'brand' describes a relation, and in particular a relation between a sign or object-image and a range of qualities it is said to index, preferably ones that invoke a positively charged affect.[2] The work of branding, then, is to establish and maintain this relation, and often find new ways to enhance or augment it, for the relation is considered the nexus of value and value-generation for the brand (Nakassis, 2013). While branding is typically employed as a marketing strategy to secure an exclusionary but dynamic form of economic value, its wider logics can apply to phenomena that may have only tangential relations with the commodity sphere.

Branded goods are familiar to consumers the world over as tangible products promoted through multi-media advertising. However, as branding is increasingly recognized as a means for generating or capturing *different* forms of value, branding activity is now used to package and distinguish collectivities and selves that do not necessarily have an obvious market function. Thus, everyday encounters with branding can be found in the work of nation-building (Jansen, 2008), in the struggle for rights and sovereignty among marginalized native and ethnic groups (Brown, 2003; Comaroff & Comaroff, 2009), and even in the intimate spaces of mourning and death (Huberman, 2013). At its heart, the concept of branding that animates such newer forms of place-branding, culture-branding, and self-branding can be distilled as the symbolic instantiation of meaningful difference – value, in other words. The logic of branding, then, is a means for congealing value under a set of signifiers and associations (both material and intangible) and thus creating a site for its subsequent extraction. Following Coombe (1998, p. 56), 'the value of a product … lies in the exchange value of its brand name, advertising image, or status connotations: the "distinction" it has, or will acquire, in the market'. More specifically, branding seeks to harness *different* kinds of value, and mobilize this collection under a banner of semiotic coherence that maintains a link to, but can travel beyond, a particular material instantiation or commodity form (Foster, 2007). In this scenario, constant effort is required to stabilize difference under a brand such that it maintains its status as an exclusive site for the reproduction of value.

Of course, tourism is no stranger to branding. The work of image making, destination crafting, logos, and slogans have long made tourism and branding intimate partners in attempts to channel value through the production of difference and distinction (Cai et al., 2009; Geary, 2013). It is from this position that I adopt the concept of brand and use it to explore dimensions of value at play in archaeological tourism at Copán, including how the ancient Maya, as a distinguished subject of archaeological and tourism interest, works as its own locus of value. Though there are current examples of corporate brand sponsorship for archaeological excavation and heritage tourism destinations in many parts of the world, this form of commercial inter-penetration is not yet common in Honduras. Instead, I concentrate here on how the logic of branding saturates the Copán context, operating in both explicit ways and as an implicit organizing principle. This case helps focus discussion on the many different dimensions of branding that inhere in heritage sites, and, subsequently, the consequences for how such complexes of value are negotiated beyond the market.

Branding Copán

Branding the past recently came to the fore in the context of celebrations hosted by Copán Ruinas, the small town adjacent to the archaeological site of Copán, in the lead up to 21 December 2012, commemorating what was widely and mistakenly portrayed in popular media as 'the end of Maya calendar'. This date, first associated with apocalyptic prophecies in the 1960s, had garnered currency among far flung publics as a pending moment of cosmological significance (Hoopes, 2011). As the date drew near, overwhelming amounts of media attention fueled a spectacularized vision of the ancient Maya in what became known globally as the '2012 phenomenon'.[3] Like their peers across the region, those involved in the tourism sector based around Copán hoped to capitalize on the 2012 phenomenon and the spike in popular interest with all things Maya to draw a record number of tourists to the site and hopefully beyond.

In the week prior to the celebrated date, a number of professionally produced banners began cropping up, posted on telephone poles near the town's central plaza and along the short stretch of highway en route to the site itself (Figure 1). In many parts of the world, appealing public banners are now a common medium for visually encoding events and places, and they provoked few overt reactions among the local audience of Honduran residents, foreign expatriates, and various tourists. In spite of their surface familiarity, it is worth examining the qualities of these banners more closely, and in particular how they signal layered forms of branding in this tourism context. First, situated along the bottom

Figure 1.   Banner on display in town of Copán Ruinas, 2012. Photo by the author.

of each banner, a familiar bright blue and white logo announced its corporate namesake, 'Tigo', one of the largest cell phone and Internet service providers in Honduras; the Tigo logo comes easily to mind when one thinks of 'brands' in Honduras.[4] In their bid to make up for funding shortages, local event organizers had approached the company to source additional last-minute sponsorship for many of the scheduled events (Julia Sandoval, personal communication, 18 December, 2012). In return, as is customary in such arrangements, Tigo affixed its logo on the promotional banners, on flyers, on overhanging welcome signs, and eventually plastered it across nearly every other available marketing space in and around Copán Ruinas. This kind of corporate sponsorship for high-profile cultural events is increasingly common in non-commercial heritage contexts such as museum exhibitions, education initiatives, even archaeological excavations.[5] Sponsorship of the Copán 2012 events fell under Tigo's 'Integrated Marketing Communications' strategy, a suite of associations and marketing opportunities that draws on the identity of the event or social context to encourage (potential) customers to develop emotionally positive associations with the brand. The logic of such a strategy follows a neoliberal formula for profit accumulation, wherein corporate owners seek to appropriate the affective labor of consumers to increase the value of the corporate brand (Arvidsson, 2005; Coombe, 1998; Foster, 2007). Like the Tigo logo itself, this strategy underscores the most familiar contemporary forms of branding practice.

But the other kinds of branding at work in these banners were somewhat less obvious. First, there is the logo 'Copán 2012', which incorporates the Maya glyph for the 13th baktun, the ending period in the Mesoamerican Long Count calendar that occasioned the celebrations. The numerical denotation of this end date, rendered in long count style, '13.0.0.0.0', signals additional linkages to the popular appeal of Maya calendrics in 2012. These inclusions broadly associate the Copán site with the greater 2012 phenomenon, a bond that is further enhanced by the inclusion of the approximate date in the Gregorian calendar, '21-Dic 2012', which itself works as a kind of short-hand, highlighting that which the banner references as distinctive in temporal, place-based, and even cosmological terms. Silhouetted background images bring forward the Copán brand; each banner incorporated a different image of sculpture or architectural feature for which the site has become known.[6] As is common in tourism dynamics, images of these iconic features circulate informally but pervasively across diverse media contexts as place-brands: referential signs that both index place and signal its distinctive attributes (Cai, 2002).

In the banners, each layer combines with and within the others to fuse a set of associations and increase the mutual marketing potential of the individual elements. Taken together, each of these discrete sign-brands works to extrapolate and generate value from and for the others, in a recursive relationship of mutual support to harness the affective attachments that any one sign may call forth, and bundle the associative qualities together so that they might travel as a whole. Rather than diluting a brand, in tourism this form of advertising often serves to invigorate and reinforce the overall value of destinations. In this case the banners do not advertise any specific event, but call attention to the confluence of events and place, much as traditional corporate-owned brands now supersede any one product (Foster, 2007).

To some extent, these signifiers only work as brand images, if they work at all, because of the prior, multi-dimensional labor that has established them as meaningful or resonant in the first place. Some of that labor has deep roots in the place-making efforts that have transformed the Copán site into a destination. More than a century ago, Honduran and foreign governments began pouring resources into carrying out documentation, excavation, and scientific recovery that provided the baseline data and subsequent status for the site as a place of academic significance in the nascent field of Maya studies (Mortensen, 2009a). Transnational partnerships, such as that between the Honduran government and the Carnegie Institute of Washington in the 1930s, later focused on the provision of capital, labor, and intellectual resources to establish the physical infrastructure for an archaeological park, including initial reconstructions of fallen architecture and clearing brush and foliage from the site center. From the 1970s onward, multilateral loans and foreign research expeditions have furthered the symbiotic goals of research and reconstruction, and added tourism service infrastructure projects to enhance the profile of the site as a destination among foreign and national visitors alike. The details of these efforts, including the successful nomination of the site to the UNESCO World Heritage List in 1980, are elaborated elsewhere (e.g. Euraque, 2010) and offer an important window to the genesis of value and notoriety that accrues to places as a result of a long history of deliberate investments and interventions. I now turn to some more recent moments in this ongoing history to signal specific precedents of branding practice and effects which prefigure the calculations of value at work in tourism there today.

My first encounter with branding as a deliberate strategy to mediate tourism engagement at Copán took place a little over a decade ago. At that time, branding surfaced in the form of a comprehensive interpretive design plan for the Copán Archaeological Park, developed as part of updating the park's management plan in a process funded by a loan from the World Bank.[7] This project was coordinated by the Wildlife Conservation Society (WCS), an international NGO specializing in protected areas, which won the contract based on its extensive experience with management and conservation throughout Central America, including precedents at this very site (Barborak, McFarland, & Morales, 1984). WCS' successful bid highlighted the promise of *standardizing* approaches to management, considered a baseline precursor for elaborating additional architecture in the smooth running of such destinations and a distinct parallel to branding logic. 'Visitor experience' at the Copán park, a dimension largely ignored in the initial management plan (completed in 1984), was slated for special attention in this process, and became the subject of a unique subcontract with the 'Heritage Design' unit of the US National Park Service.[8]

In contemplating the overall tourism vision for Copán, Heritage Design consultants singled out the need for a 'family of signs and structures' that would contribute to the aesthetic coherence of the park and its infrastructure as a packaged destination. They explained, 'using the common design elements, the family provides a standard unified approach and look to all directional, informative and interpretive signage within the Park' (Mattson & Guarisco, 2005, p. 179). Additional recommendations for design extended the material matrix to encompass the categories of color, fonts, titles, text, artwork, and logos. The consultants also advised that 'elements are used consistently on all signs, structures, and peripheral materials to create brand recognition (or market identity) for Copán' (Mattson & Guarisco, 2005, p. 178). Taken together, this articulated the physical designates, and to some extent the rationale, for an explicit branding strategy for the Copán park. As with the more recent banners, the objective here was to cohere a suite of visual-material elements that would engender recognition among visitors both actual and potential (cf. Cai, 2002). Such a system, they argued, would create a '"sense of place" or identity for the Park' (Mattson & Guarisco, 2005, p. 179). Implicit here is the imperative, from a marketing perspective, to develop a more recognizable and potentially portable *brand* identity, since Copán's 'sense of place' was already quite well established for most visitors and residents.

The tactics of branding outlined above, familiar to the world of tourism marketing professionals, did not present as an alien imposition in the local context of archaeological tourism. For within this context the Copán park already conformed to a set of standardized expectations that make local ruins recognizable and accessible as spaces of leisure (Castañeda, 1996; Ehrentraut, 1996). For example, a range of modest structural elements differentiate the protected area from the surrounding fields, forest, and residential zones: the park boundaries are demarcated by a fence line, visitors purchase tickets from a ticket booth, and enter by way of a zoned parking area flanked on either end by a visitor center and gift shop (Figure 2). A groomed path then leads from the cluster of service buildings through a dense patch of shady tropical forest, delivering visitors into a dazzlingly bright and manicured plaza where reconstructed monuments of the ancient city center have been consolidated and cleared for modern forms of tourist consumption (Figure 3). Individual guides or portable guidebooks direct visitors along pathways among fallen architectural mounds covered with moss, shrubs, and budding trees, and offer narratives highlighting the elaborate artwork and stone sculpture that have been carefully conserved in situ or re-positioned in the on-site museum. These elements, practices, and forms, replicated across similar sites throughout the region, operate as an incipient and subtle form of branding, marking the site among its peers as a proper 'Maya archaeological tourism' destination (Castañeda & Mathews, 2013; Mortensen, 2009b), a form key to the successful transnational tourism circuit 'La Ruta Maya', and thus very difficult to disrupt (Euraque, 2010; Joyce, 2013).

Features that distinguish the Copán site within the greater field of archaeological heritage, such as an architectural structure known as the 'hieroglyphic stairway', which boasts the single longest carved text in the Americas, were critical factors that contributed to its formal designation as a UNESCO World Heritage Site in 1980. This designation, though ostensibly removed from commercial activity, confers upon the site a status (or 'value') that operates according to brand logics as well (DiGiovine, 2009). With World Heritage status comes the obligation for sites to conform to a UNESCO 'standard certification of authenticity and quality', conditions that are subsequently communicated to potential publics through the selective right to use the World Heritage emblem.[9] Following more conventional brand practice, UNESCO retains proprietary control over its emblem, a

Figure 2.   Entrance to the Copán Archaeological Park, 2012. Photo by the author.

Figure 3.   Great Plaza of the Copán Archaeological Park, 2007. Photo by the author.

trademarked symbol protected under the World Intellectual Property Organization from unauthorized uses (though, to date, policing of the brand is rarely enforced by institutional agents) (DiGiovine, 2009). While the UNESCO World Heritage List is meant to single out tangible and intangible legacies that warrant special protections because they represent transcendent cultural value, increasingly that value is being realized and recognized in economic terms, aiding states to compete in 'an increasingly acquisitive heritage economy' (Meskell, 2014, p. 237; see also Kirshenblatt-Gimblett, 2006).

By the standards of North American heritage marketing professionals in 2001, the extant forms of branding described above for Copán, even buttressed by UNESCO's emblem, were still lacking. In particular, the modest signage that accompanied the park layout was considered insufficient to properly communicate the distinction and identity of this place, as well as its broader connection to the surrounding physical and social land-scape. Planners identified this as a lacunae within which increased place-value lay in-poten-tia, a key opportunity to better link symbolic and economic value through a comprehensive visual-material palette. This precipitated the focus on 'design elements' as a domain for identity elaboration, both within the park (as noted already) and also beyond:

> Uniform design elements should be used on all Park information and interpretation: media for the valley, archaeological zone and towns. Designs should be organic and as indigenous as possible. They should enhance, but not compete with or imitate the ruins. These designs should tie in everything from on-the-ground information and interpretive signage, to collateral materials such as brochures, and website marketing efforts. (Mattson & Guarisco, 2005, p. 178)

Copán branding extended

Two short years later, in 2003, a next and more massive iteration of World Bank funding for the 'Regional Development of the Copán Valley Project' (PDRVC)[10] provided direct support for putting these recommendations into effect. Unlike the previous management plan project, in which tourism figured only as one extension of the park's overall operations, this new loan centered on developing the regional tourism market, based loosely around the park as just one component. Guided by the core goal of 'sustainable tourism development based on the cultural and natural patrimony of the Copán Valley', the PDRVC project envisioned a range of activities, including technical assistance for tourism service/product development, capacity building for employment in tourism and heritage management sectors, and support for strategic tourism planning among community, private, and public stakeholders. One of the most tangible results of this coordinated approach was an effort to extend the park-based branding effects to encompass the entire region, and organize the experience of destination under even more sensory logics.

These efforts became the responsibility of a new 'Municipal Urban Planning Office', eventually located within the administrative center of Copán Ruinas, whose mandate was to elaborate 'a unique urban design scheme for the preservation of the colonial legacy' of Copán Ruinas, backed by 'the authority to review, approve and monitor the execution of new constructions and rehabilitations of civil works, in order to ensure that they were in harmony with the proposed urban design concept' (World Bank, 2010, p. 19). According to the principles guiding the project, specific elements of the 'design plan should emerge from truly local concepts of place and experience'. To this end, a US Peace Corps volunteer assigned to the office carried out focus group studies with members of the community, different local associations, schools, and professional organizations, soliciting input on what the planners should look to as foundational sources of aesthetic inspiration. Perhaps not surprisingly, many of the sources suggested were linked to core aspects of distinctiveness that already circulated in the tourism image of town and site, and specifically those with some conceived link to the ancient Maya. One palette drawn up was based on the colors encountered on remnants of painted stucco preserved on the entombed temple known as 'Rosalila' discovered beneath the site's tallest architectural complex and recreated in full color in the on-site Copán Sculpture Museum (Figure 4). Another referenced the spectacular array of hues in 'guacamayas', or scarlet macaws, rationalized by the designers as a 'representative element of the Maya culture'. In addition to the recommended color schemes, the plan and subsequent regulations sought to govern a near-comprehensive array of architectural features and details in the town of Copán Ruinas, ranging in scope from the size, shape, and style of buildings and their materials, down to recommended types of specific windows, balconies, and doors (Figure 5). Most importantly to the architects of the project, signage of all forms was to be strictly controlled.

In disseminating information about the new regulations, and encouraging buy-in by local residents, office staff carefully stopped short of more punitive means of compliance. Instead they focused on a 'socialization' campaign to 'change the habits' of residents and emphasize the value-potential in the collective project of transforming the town's image. Individuals contemplating new construction or renovation were encouraged to visit the municipal office with photos of their buildings and consider the professionally assembled color palette. The project leader emphasized their operating mode, 'No one says you have to paint, but *if* you paint, then choose one of these colors' (Carlotta Valladares, personal communication, 20 June, 2007). Computer-generated virtual reconstructions of houses allowed home and business owners to preview their private spaces remade under the more uniform aesthetic. Office staff began posting public messages of thanks on the town's cable channel acknowledging those who adopted the new colors and styles, hoping to spur greater ripple effects.

Figure 4.   "Rosalila" temple in the Copan Sculpture Museum, Copán Archaeological Park, Honduras 2007. Photo by the author.

The campaign to standardize the town image, backed by planners, funders, and heritage professionals, resonated with the parameters of destination management but also spoke to the sense of community distinction and civic identity that place-branding efforts routinely espouse (Anholt, 2009). Pleas for residents to conform to new aesthetic norms were underwritten by the conviction that an 'authentic' place-based identity can be apprehended and expressed in material form, and that maintaining continuity in such expression is reciprocally beneficial to both outsiders and residents.[11] Thus, residents were admonished to 'not use elements that are not ours', especially after planners had gone to so much trouble to formally elicit that which might be embraced under a collective symbolic identity.

A report from 2004 lauds the perceived successes partway through the project: 'In two years, this support has helped give Copán Ruinas a brand new image, while expanding income generation opportunities for its poor inhabitants and increasing their sense of local heritage and distinctiveness.'[12] In this scenario, a 'brand new image' (though already a contentious claim) can also be read as a *branded* new image. The standardization of visual aesthetics here implicates building brand value along several dimensions. First, there is the effort to better link Copán Ruinas, the town and region, to the central attraction of the Copán park through a visual code based on a shared sense of archaeological heritage (based around the ancient Maya) and colonial history. This process folds the region under

46

Figure 5.   Street scene in Copán Ruinas, Honduras, 2012. Photo by the author.

the Copán brand while encouraging a distinctive civic identity based on that linkage. The signage projects and related urban planning initiatives were, in fact, expressly conceived as a means for the local town to better benefit from the tourist attention and symbolic notoriety the site already garnered. Here, branding operates as a way of extracting more value from the attraction that is seen as the primary locus of profit generation. In branding logic, without a unifying way of signifying the association, the transfer of capital is unstable. Establishing and securing such linkages is what makes this kind of connection and value transfer complete.

Branding and beyond

It would be easy at this point to cynically dismiss or condemn the deliberate engineering of place and experience targeted through these planning developments as just another form of tourism manufacturing that alienates people from an authentic heritage. But there are more fundamental dynamics of branding at work here that seek to circumscribe value at yet another scale in this configuration, and these, too, beg examination. The more recent work of physical branding at Copán, and the capital available for its realization through multi-million dollar bi-lateral loans, are built on and prefigured by the overarching brand value of Maya archaeology and the Copán product in particular. The language of 'product' is deliberate, and replicates how staff in the Honduran Institute of Tourism (IHT) formally, and without irony, conceptualize Copán: as one of the country's most readily marketable 'Tourism Products'. In the ontology employed by IHT, tourism products are country-based destinations that are 'ready' for the market. In this formulation as a product, Copán figures as a key resource that can be sold across borders, circulating precisely through some of the forms of branding logic already referenced above. According to international surveys conducted by IHT staff, Copán already registers positively in the international imagination (unlike the nation-brand of Honduras more generally). Thus, opportunities to further invest in the Copán brand, to extend associations, and to develop more products under its name continue to attract interest on the part of entrepreneurs, government organizations, private institutions, lending agencies, and myriad others seeking to extract value from its securely bundled constellation of qualities.[13]

Harvey (2002) has signaled the growing significance of local cultural specificity as a strategy for capturing monopoly rents and it is this dynamic that underwrites the logic of branding at play in the Copán context. Drawing on Bourdieu, Harvey frames this quality of distinction as 'collective symbolic value', the translation of which results in an ever-widening array of cultural forms as commodities. Key here, as discussed above, is the ability to trade on cultural distinction as a means for market advantage in arenas such as tourism, urban development, and cultural industries more generally. The dynamics of place branding help secure this distinction in ways similar to how 'marks of origin' help generate value for cultural commodities (Coombe & Aylwin, 2011), by delineating a set of associations that constitute the essential or 'authentic' cultural form. Though the informal branding practices at Copán operate without the architecture of legal protections that circumscribe some such cultural commodities, the logic of branding still works to create distinction that can be traded upon as an important source of value.

It is in this way that the 'ancient Maya', as an archaeological subject and highly marketable commodity, also acts as a kind of brand, and one which, in a distinctly recursive relationship, over 100 years of high profile research at Copán has helped to build. Ancient Maya 'things', particularly the showy material legacy upon which archaeological tourism is based, constitute an anchor for the brand, but so do the tropes, images, and desires now deeply associated with this cultural form (Castañeda, 1996; Hervik, 2003; Lerner, 2011).[14] In the economy of signs that reference cultural pasts it is clear that the ancient Maya have significant brand value.[15] This was made evident throughout the year 2012, as museums, universities, whole countries, towns, and sites sought to highlight some subset of their related resources, connecting with and hoping to extract value from the brand.

This returns us to the banners referenced toward the beginning of this discussion. Notably absent from the bundle of signs on the banners is any overt reference to Honduras. As referenced earlier, nation-branding is now a signature tool in neoliberal governance through which countries exercise soft-power, appealing to foreign investment as well as tourist receipts (e.g. Jansen, 2008). But in Honduras, the work of nation-branding is incomplete. Since the coup d'état that took place in 2009, the brand, as it were, has been in particular peril (not unjustifiably due to an escalating crime-rate, violence, political corruption, and human rights abuses). However, despite coordinated efforts especially on the part of the National Tourism Ministry, the country struggled to project a positive image long before the political crisis.[16] However successfully linked Copán and Maya appear to be, there has always been slippage when Honduras is added to the brand equation. Efforts to harmonize this fusion have often resulted in a conflict of affects wherein the potential for mutual synergy is disrupted. Consequently, the Copán Maya brand is routinely oriented away from the political present of its troubled host country, emphasizing instead a timeless tourist space that dissolves both territorial and temporal borders into a stylized past, materialized through the many markers referenced above.

Futures of branding the past

The logics of branding, as I have described them in relation to place-making and value-making at Copán, are pervasive. I dwell on them here not to celebrate this trend, but to raise it up for scrutiny. The ways in which branding serves to organize resources under particular signs or cultural forms – delimiting value for narrow sets of experience, lived space, narratives of heritage, and, ultimately, cultural subjects – deserve much more attention, and the case I have presented here only begins to scratch the surface. But it is also clear that there are limits to this frame of analysis in how branding may ultimately subsume heritage tourism contexts. This is best illustrated through the primary difference between corporate brands, where ownership (and therefore the means to extract rent and collect profit) lies in the hands of shareholders and private investors who realize direct profit from the activities of the corporation, and culture-as-brand, where ownership, at least in a capitalist market sense, is most often diffuse and rarely regulated through traditional juridical means.[17] And this is where the potential to contest and subvert brand logics ultimately lies. At Copán, all the physical work of place-branding, with its careful planning by design specialists, city officials, and tourism professionals, does not operate in the same manner of aligning commodity products with their corporate brand owners. Instead, the smoothing attempts of place-branding rub up against the unsanctioned actions of those subjects who populate and constitute place. Though I have not covered them in any detail here, the selective responses of unruly subjects (resident citizen-actors) to the branding practices and logics at Copán have the power to fundamentally and productively disrupt that which branding seeks to establish as coherent, and re-establish non-branded claims to the living values of place.

For the most part, Copán has thus far eluded the contentious struggles that characterize the playing field of intellectual property rights with respect to cultural commodities (Coombe, 1998). But it may be that such a future is not far off. While there is as yet no strict 'owner' of Copán as a brand, as a branded destination, or of the ancient Maya in general, there are most certainly descendants whose claim to this cultural legacy raises a distinct set of considerations in the field of heritage values, let alone heritage rights (Silverman & Ruggles, 2008). Contemporary Maya peoples have long struggled to position their voice and needs against the dominant tourist portrayal of their heritage. Like the now incorporated Zulu nation in South Africa (Comaroff & Comaroff, 2009), might they also begin considering options to license a claim to monopoly benefits accruing from renting out their association with their highly marketable past? Might other forces counter such potential claims by moving to formalize the incipient branding already at work at Copán and similar heritage tourism contexts? Such possibilities of action in 'making difference meaningful' require that we keep a close eye on the evolution of branding the past and its relationship to not only the complex of value, but, more importantly, to the cultural subjects whom it most closely implicates and affects.

Notes

1. This article is based on ethnographic research by the author with archaeological tourism and heritage management at the site of Copán, and in Honduras more generally, in intermittent periods from 1998 to 2012.
2. See Manning (2010) for an overview of recent critical scholarship on branding in anthropology and related disciplines.
3. This phenomenon developed in spite of the many efforts of scholars and contemporary Maya to debunk the notion that the Long Count calendar was set to 'end' rather than simply turn over a new cycle.
4. Tigo is in turn part of an international brand owned by the corporation Millicom, a telecommunications and digital service company with commercial operations throughout Latin America and Africa.

5. See, for example, the list of corporate sponsors associated with excavations at the World Heritage Site of Catalhöyük in Turkey (http://www.catalhoyuk.com/).
6. The banner pictured in Figure 1 features Copán's famous hieroglyphic staircase.
7. The new management plan was part of a larger US$8.3 million World Bank-funded project, 'PROFUTURO' (World Bank, 2006).
8. I participated as an informal observer throughout the duration of this process.
9. However, recent research among tourism scholars demonstrates that popular recognition of the World Heritage brand remains limited (King & Halpenny, 2014).
10. World Bank project ID# P081172.
11. It should be noted that while place-branding rhetorically promises civic pride and enhanced quality of living, these are secondary to the market logic that drives the process.
12. Copan Valley Regional Sustainable Tourism and Cultural Heritage Project: An Innovative Approach to Poverty Reduction and Local Development from Central America, p. 7, retrieved from http://siteresources.worldbank.org/INTLAC/Resources/Copan_Results.pdf.
13. The value of this name brand is so securely tied to its referent that any alterations to the name or its extensions are seen as threatening that value. Thus, a recent proposition by Honduran president Porfirio Lobo in 2012 to change the town's name from Copán Ruinas to Copán Galel, in honor of a sixteenth-century indigenous leader, was resoundingly rejected by local residents and the business community more generally.
14. These studies offer detailed accounts of how ideas about the 'mysterious Maya' have long penetrated the North American public imagination, and continue to circulate through a wide array of media channels.
15. Note that this concept of an archaeological subject as 'brand' is distinct from how Holtorf (2007) argues that 'archaeology is a brand', and his calls for professionals to embrace the positive popular appeal the discipline enjoys.
16. A detailed discussion of the halting business of nation-building through nation-branding in Honduras is beyond the scope of the present article.
17. However, this distinction is also increasingly porous. For discussion of the recent proliferation of legally branded and incorporated cultural collectivities in North America and Southern Africa, see, for example, Comaroff and Comaroff (2009).

References

Anderson, M. (2013). Notes on tourism, ethnicity and the politics of cultural value in Honduras. In B. Hogenboom, J. Burrell, & E. Moodie (Eds.), *Central America in the new millennium: Living transition and reimagining democracy* (pp. 276–293). New York, NY: Berghahn.

Anholt, S. (2009). *Places: Identity, image and reputation*. New York, NY: Palgrave Macmillan.

Appadurai, A. (1994). Commodities and the politics of value. In S. Pearce (Ed.), *Interpreting objects and collections* (pp. 76–91). London: Routledge.

Arvidsson, A. (2005). Brands: A critical perspective. *Journal of Consumer Culture, 5*(2), 235–258.

Askew, M. (2010). The magic list of global status: UNESCO, World Heritage and the agendas of states. In S. Labadi & C. Long (Eds.), *Heritage and globalisation* (pp. 19–44). London: Routledge.

Barborak, J., McFarland, C., & Morales, R. (1984). *Plan de manejo y desarollo del Monumento Nacional Ruinas de Copán*. Turrialba: UNESCO, IHAH y CATIE.

Brown, M. (2003). *Who owns native culture?* Cambridge, MA: Harvard University Press.

Cai, L. (2002). Cooperative branding for rural destinations. *Annals of Tourism Research, 29*(3), 720–742.

Cai, L., Gartner, W., & Munar, A. (Eds.). (2009). *Tourism branding: Communities in action*. Bingley: Emerald Group.

Castañeda, Q. (1996). *In the museum of Maya culture: Touring Chichén Itzá*. Minneapolis: University of Minnesota Press.

Castañeda, Q., & Matthews, J. (2013). Archaeology Meccas of tourism: Exploration, protection, exploitation/life on the 'B list'. In C. Walker & N. Carr (Eds.), *Tourism and archaeology: Sustainable meeting grounds* (pp. 37–64). Walnut Creek, CA: Left Coast.

Comaroff, J., & Comaroff, J. (2009). *Ethnicity, Inc.* Chicago, IL: Chicago University Press.

Coombe, R. (1998). *The cultural life of intellectual properties: Authorship, appropriation, and the law*. Durham, NC: Duke University Press.

Coombe, R., & Aylwin, N. (2011). Bordering diversity and desire: Using intellectual property to mark place-based products. *Environment and Planning A, 43*(9), 2027–2042.

Dallen, T., & Boyd, S. (2006). Heritage tourism in the 21st century: Valued traditions and new perspectives. *Journal of Heritage Tourism, 1*(1), 1–16.

DiGiovine, M. (2009). *The heritage-scape: UNESCO, World Heritage, and tourism.* Lanham, MD: Lexington Books.

Ehrentraut, A. (1996). Maya ruins, cultural tourism, and the contested symbolism of collective identities. *Culture, 16*(1), 15–32.

Eiss, P., & Pedersen, D. (2002). Introduction: Values of value. *Cultural Anthropology, 17*(3), 283–290.

Euraque, D. (2010). *El Golpe de estado del 28 de Junio de 2009, el patrimonio cultural y la identidad nacional de Honduras.* San Pedro Sula: Centro Impresora.

Ferry, E. (2013). *Minerals, collecting, and value across the US-Mexico border.* Bloomington: Indiana University Press.

Foster, R. J. (2007). The work of the new economy: Consumers, brands, and value creation. *Cultural Anthropology, 22*(4), 707–731.

Geary, D. (2013). Incredible India in a global age: The cultural politics of image branding in tourism. *Tourist Studies, 13*(1), 36–61.

Goldman, R., & Papson, S. (2006). Capital's brandscapes. *Journal of Consumer Culture, 6*(3), 327–353.

Graeber, D. (2001). *Towards an anthropological theory of value.* New York, NY: Palgrave.

Harvey, D. (2002). The art of rent: Globalisation, monopoly and the commodification of culture. *Socialist Register, 38*, 93–110.

Hervik, P. (2003). *Mayan people within and beyond boundaries: Social categories and lived identity in Yucatán.* New York, NY: Routledge.

Holtorf, C. (2007). *Archaeology is a brand!: The meaning of archaeology in contemporary popular culture.* Walnut Creek, CA: Left Coast.

Hoopes, J. (2011). A critical history of 2012 mythology. *Proceedings of the International Astronomical Union, 7*(S278), 240–248.

Huberman, J. (2013). Forever a fan: Reflections on the branding of death and the production of value. *Anthropological Theory, 12*(4), 467–485.

Jansen, S. (2008). Designer nations: Neo-liberal nation branding – Brand Estonia. *Social Identities, 14*(1), 121–142.

Joyce, R. (2013). Confessions of an archaeological tour guide. *International Journal of Historical Archaeology, 17*(2), 296–314.

King, L., & Halpenny, E. (2014). Communicating the World Heritage brand: Visitor awareness of UNESCO's World Heritage symbol and the implications for sites, stakeholders and sustainable management. *Journal of Sustainable Tourism, 22*(5), 768–786.

Kirshenblatt-Gimblett, B. (2006). World Heritage and cultural economics. In I. Karp, C. Kratz, L. Szwaja, & T. Ybarra-Frausto (Eds.), *Museum frictions: Public cultures/global transformations* (pp. 161–202). Durham, NC: Duke University Press.

Lerner, J. (2011). *The Maya of modernism: Art, architecture, and film.* Santa Fe: University of New Mexico Press.

Lowenthal, D. (1986). *The past is a foreign country.* Cambridge: Cambridge University Press.

Manning, P. (2010). The semiotics of brand. *Annual Review of Anthropology, 39*, 33–49.

Mattson, D., & Guarisco, J. (2005). Interpretive concepts for Copan Archaeological Park. In *Plan de manejo: Zona arqueológica de Copán* (Anexo 13, pp. 173–187). Tegucigalpa: IHAH.

Meskell, L. (2014). States of conservation: Protection, politics, and pacting within UNESCO's World Heritage Committee. *Anthropological Quarterly, 87*(1), 217–243.

Miller, D. (2008). The uses of value. *Geoforum, 39*, 1122–1132.

Mortensen, L. (2009a). Producing Copán in the archaeology industry. In L. Mortensen & J. Hollowell (Eds.), *Ethnographies and archaeologies: Iterations of the past* (pp. 178–198). Gainesville: University Press of Florida.

Mortensen, L. (2009b). Copán past and present: Maya archaeological tourism and the Ch'orti' in Honduras. In B. Metz, C. McNeil, & K. Hull (Eds.), *The Ch'orti' region, past and present* (pp. 246–257). Gainesville: University Press of Florida.

Nakassis, C. V. (2013). Brands and their surfeits. *Cultural Anthropology, 28*(1), 111–126.

Scher, P. W. (2011). Heritage tourism in the Caribbean: The politics of culture after neoliberalism. *Bulletin of Latin American Research, 30*(1), 7–20.

Silverman, H., & Ruggles, D. F. (2008). Cultural heritage and human rights. In H. Silverman & D. F. Ruggles (Eds.), *Cultural heritage and human rights* (pp. 3–29). New York, NY: Springer.

Smith, G., Messenger, P., & Soderland, H. (Eds.). (2010). *Heritage values in contemporary society.* Walnut Creek, CA: Left Coast.

World Bank. (2006). *Honduras – interactive environmental learning and science promotion project* (Report No. 35652). Washington, DC: Author.

World Bank. (2010). *Honduras – regional development in the Copan Valley Project* (Report No. ICR0000899). Washington, DC: Author.

Yudice, G. (2003). *The expediency of culture: The uses of culture in the global era.* Durham, NC: Duke University Press.

Values of property (properties of value): capitalization of kinship in Norway

Simone Abram[a,b]

[a]International Centre for Research in Events, Tourism and Hospitality, Leeds Met University, UK;
[b]Department of Anthropology, Durham University, UK

This paper examines the multiple forms of value invested in holiday properties among some Norwegian families. Holiday homes – summer houses, mountain cabins and country houses – are common in Norway, as are many of the practices through which they are inhabited, shared and inherited. Within the legal practices of testaments and handovers can be found a wealth of kinds of value, some of which can be translated into each other. For example, the capitalization of ownership and use for the purposes of inheritance concretize the relations between family members in both financial and emotional terms. In exploring these relations, this paper considers the connections between people, property, landscape and movement through time.

On regimes and on value

The title of this volume, Regimes of Value, points to Appadurai's (1986) thesis on the complexity of relations of economic value and exchange value. Appadurai builds on Simmel's observation that value is constituted by the exchange of an object, not by the object itself. Where Simmel goes on to discuss the role of money in exchange and value, Appadurai takes the anthropological route to consider different contexts in which objects circulate and the specifics of the creation of value in these different contexts, which he names 'regimes of value'. Appadurai was predominantly concerned with material objects and their exchange, contemplating Marxist ideas about the 'spirit of the commodity' and noting the tendency in anthropological writing to continue to set two types of exchange into opposition – gift exchange and commodity exchange. The contributors to Appadurai's book offer detailed discussions of the journey of objects in and out of the role of commodity, where value and price can become untethered, and where inter-cultural contexts generate situations where values are not shared between the parties to an exchange. Inevitably, in an anthropological discussion of exchange and gifts, the question arises of the Kula exchange system of the Western Pacific, a case that has been closely investigated and extensively discussed since Malinowski's classic account (1922). In brief (exceedingly brief), Kula is a system for exchanging shell valuables where valuables circulate between owners, gaining biographical richness and substance as they move between owners. The important facet of this exchange system of note here is the way in which the holding of a Kula valuable brings reputation to the holder. That is, not only does the object gain value in its route of exchange, but the owner also gains and loses value in the cycle of receiving, owning and giving (see Munn, 1986; Weiner, 1976). There is a corollary of sorts among European monarchies – the monarch owns the crown of glittering worth, but ownership of the crown confers royalty upon the monarch, and the monarch thus grows in value through owning the valuable item. Of course, to add a level of complexity, as with Kula shells, a crown need not be a particularly valuable item in itself – although gold and jewels add a dimension of commercial cost and exclusivity to its value – but its symbolic value as an item that may only be owned by the monarch is what brings value to the monarch in his or her own person. In this sense, an object may confer value onto a person.

The relationship between this symbolic value that is attributable to ownership and the monetary value of an object is complex and provides the basic ethnographic conundrum to the articles in Appadurai's volume. It further provokes a discussion between Otto and Willerslev (2013) on the potential for anthropological discussion about exchange relations to generate a general anthropological theory of value. They take up Dumont's question of comparing different value systems and assert that action is both informed by value and creates value. In other words, through different kinds of actions (including exchanges) an object may accrue value or lose it or change the kind of value that it has. Tsing's (2013) ethnography of Matsutaki mushrooms, for example, demonstrates the stages through which objects are commoditized through depersonalizing the relations between the mushroom and the owner (conversion into priceable and salable commodities), before repersonalization as they are purchased as gifts. The work of sorting mushrooms removes them from one set of personal relations (the 'hunter' finding the mushroom in the woods) and enables them to be recontextualized into another set of personal relations (gift-giving). More explicit accounts are also available of the tension between commercial (financial) value, and ethical, social or environmental value (see Dalsgaard, 2013; Ortiz, 2013), demonstrating that monetary value is one of a range of values that can accrue and disperse from particular objects, including imaginary objects, through time and through changing relations of exchange and ownership of the object. Ownership is a crucial element of exchange that has often been overshadowed by an emphasis on the exchange relation in anthropology, but has recently returned (Strang & Busse, 2011). That ownership is a 'shadow concept' (Strathern, 2011) of exchange is a peculiar but important notion in relation to value. Value, in other words, is fluid, multidimensional, sometimes fleeting and tied to action (of which exchange is one example).

In this paper, two fields of value are explicated that are among many related to property in the form of owned, built dwellings. Property is a particularly vexing object of value, since the values attributed to property range from symbolic and emotional to the exemplary instance of flawed market exchange. Housing was at the core of the 2008 financial crash, through the selling of virtualized credit, generating a huge financial bubble that collapsed in the most dramatic fashion. Housing market bubbles fuel housing problems across Europe, with price and use-value diverging wildly in many locations, with serious consequences for people unable to afford inflated rents or prices, just as much as for those left with unsalable assets in unfashionable locations (for a lively account, see Meek, 2014). At the same time, homes are more than just dwellings, providing both the location and the material of family life, facilitating particular relations and materializing others (see Carsten & Hugh-Jones, 2004). Homes can be bought and sold, certainly, and they may be gifted – in particular they may be inherited in a special form of gift-giving, as I will outline below – and they may also be split and shared. In other words, houses are an extremely mutable form of property that requires people to reconcile conflicting forms of value. In this paper, I offer a short ethnographic example of one method through which attempts are made to reconcile conflicting registers of value and in the process constructing a new regime of value, in the context of holiday-making (a form of tourism).

Holiday homes as property with properties

This paper addresses the uses and ownership of Norwegian holiday homes, often designated as 'second homes'.[1] Second homes are increasingly acknowledged as an important form of tourism, accounting for a significant sector of leisure travel, production and consumption (see Gallent & Tewdwr-Jones, 2000).

Literature on second homes has acknowledged in two ways that not all second homes are merely market commodities: firstly, by focusing intensely on the meaning and significance of a second home in the leisure life of the occupiers (Hall & Muller, 2004), and secondly, in acknowledging that second homes in some circumstances are inherited rather than bought and sold (Kaltenborn, 1998). Less attention has been focused on how this works in practice and how the practices of inheritance shape second home use and ownership. As with all homes, second homes also have market value, whatever their emotional significance, and given the centrality of the tension between market and affect in Western social life, it is not surprising to see it reproduced in the field of second homes.

Flognfeldt (2004) estimates that up to half of the Norwegian population has access to a holiday home, and it is clear that a significant proportion of the population own either one or several such homes, either outright or in common with others. It is relatively unusual in Norway for adults to move into the primary home of a deceased parent (other than on farms), but it is common to occupy an inherited holiday home. Research on the forms and practices of ownership and transference of these homes can reveal who owns holiday homes, who inherits them and who does not inherit. This, in turn, can tell us much about the ways that holiday home properties are used to 'kin' relatives, and how distinctions between kinds of relatives are made. Ownership signifies a complex web of relations, which both forms and reforms kinship relations, as well as having economic and socio-political significance. One might say that holiday homes are involved in both kinning and de-kinning Norwegian families. This paper represents a small project on second home practices in Norway, which addresses the movements and activities related to the holiday home (see Abram, 2012; Ween & Abram, 2012), and the ownership of the property. It is based on visits to cabins, informal discussions with a range of cabin owners, interviews with solicitors, examination of a selection of legal files and a review of court records. The paper outlines the regimes of value associated with Norwegian holiday homes by paying attention to inheritance.

Kinning and houses

Anthropological research on kinship is largely concerned with the ways in which particular relations are identified and enacted on, through practices such as naming, exchanges, as well as reproductive practices. It starts from the premise that different societies tend to acknowledge different kinds of relations in different ways as kin relations, whether that be the identification of all maternal siblings in maternal relations with a child, the letting go of categories of cousin through underemphasis (through scalar effects: first cousins → second cousins → distant relations) or the wide variety of extended kin structures, such as clan or exclusively matrilateral or patrilateral kinship systems. The point is that kinship relations, far from simply existing as genealogical (let along biological) ties, are relations that are practiced, given meaning or cultivated in a partial and ongoing way.

Howell (2006) defines kinning as 'the process by which a foetus or newborn child is brought into a significant and permanent relationship with a group of people, and the connection is expressed in a conventional kin idiom' (p. 8). She permits that kinning 'need not apply only to a baby, but to any previously unconnected person, such as those connected by marriage'. Howells argues elsewhere that the study of adoption, that is, explicit kinning activities, shed light on what we might think of as 'normal' kinship, through the contrast it offers. In particular, she is interested in how non-biological kinship offers a reflection on the biologism that is otherwise inherent in Western kinship concepts. Howell is concerned with transnational adoption and the different status that adopted children have to immigrant children, particularly the ways they are included into a (metaphorical) Norwegian national family. However, it is possible to extend Howell's idea about kinning through reference to Carsten's work on kinship, inspired by Levi-Strauss's work on House Societies, as follows.

In House Societies, relations are defined by the material and immaterial estate that constitutes a 'family' and is signified by the house and property of the estate. In conceptualizing the estate, Levi-Strauss was thinking of the historic noble houses of Europe, where estates including land, noble titles and built property were passed on through firstborns from grandfather to grandson. But Carsten and Hugh-Jones (2004) have applied the principle to other societies where the sharing of substance and space is integral to reproducing kin relations. According to Carsten, Levi-Strauss's discussion of Indonesian society suggested that neither filiation, property, nor residence alone constitute kinship groups, but that marriage both unites families and provides tension between them. She outlines how, when a married couple leave their respective places of residence and form a new house, this new house and the children born to it appear to solidify the relations between the couple, over and above the relations to their respective kin (p.106). That is, the construction of a marital household can be crucial to the formation of a marriage and its consolidation through the birth of children and the establishment of a new family. Whereas Bourdieu's description of the Kabyle house saw it as a reflection or representation of the gendered domestic relations played out within and around it, Maurice Bloch suggests that the house physically becomes the core of a marital unit rather than merely representing it (Bloch, 2004). Among Bloch's Zafimanary informants, newly married couples begin to build a rudimentary house, and over time it 'hardens' through the addition of solid building materials, and increasingly elaborate carvings on the main supporting posts. Such houses are passed on to youngest sons, but eventually, as subsequent sons leave to form their own households, it becomes a holy house at which blessings are made by later generations to the original ancestor couple who built the house. In other words, the house gradually becomes an arena for and the object of kinship rituals, thereby constituting kinship itself.

One might thus argue that the house itself becomes a means of kinning, providing the context and inspiration for the practice of kinship relations among affines, parents, children, siblings, etc. As will become clear, the greatest contrast between this and the case of Norwegian holiday homes is in the role of marriage as opposed to siblingship or parenthood. This is most clearly apparent through an examination of inheritance practices, as outlined below.

Norwegian cabins and the excess of emotion

While there are many different categories of holiday home in Norway, the term 'hytte' covers many of them, and here I will use the English term Cabin in its place. They may be mountain cabins, seaside summer houses or old farms in the woods, but what unites them is their use as family holiday homes, their occupation during a limited number of weeks in each year and their location out of the city, even if only a short distance. What distinguishes them is particularly the experience that many people share, of spending regular holidays at the cabin throughout their childhood along with their closest family members, of playing in and around the cabin over many years, exploring the surrounding territory through hiking, skiing or trekking and associated activities (fishing, building fires and picnicking) and the emotional intensity that this brings in relation to the particular place and the people with whom it is shared. At the cabin, people often spend time making their own fittings, bringing particular stones or pieces of wood from the surrounding area to the cabin site, or making decorations, as well as in customizing bought items to suit their needs or desires.[2] Such home-made items are thus invested with shared experience and historical significance, and often become the focus of sentiment and nostalgia.[3] The home-made may also include the cabin itself, or its fittings and furnishings, and these add to the emotional intensity related to the cabin that often comes to the fore in the process of inheritance (see Abram, 2012). The most common first response that many Norwegian correspondents give to my description of the cabin research I am embarking on is, 'oh, so many feelings'. Many of these feelings come to a head when a cabin is passed on from one generation to the next, or sold out of the family. Almost every Norwegian whom I have asked about inheritance has been able to refer to at least one family who has been traumatized by conflicts over the inheritance of a cabin. In other words, this is a common experience, and thus worthy of detailed attention.

Norwegian inheritance in law and practice

Norwegian inheritance law is based on partible inheritance (similar to French inheritance practice, for example) and is focused primarily on parenthood and siblingship. Married couples share property in common and therefore do not 'inherit' from each other the property that they already own together. In contrast, the death of a surviving spouse triggers the inheritance of the property shared between the couple to their heirs, although this can also be precipitated in advance of death. In the law, inheritance follows a hierarchical schedule, with children and grandchildren being first in line (referred to in law as in the first class), with the deceased's parents and their other children (the deceased's siblings) in second class and grandparents and their children (deceased's cousins – parents' siblings children) in third class. Within the second class, inheritance follows branches, with older generations inheriting first, before their children, and each branch's share divided between heirs in subsequent generations (Figure 1). In this generational hierarchy, half-siblings may inherit through their respective parents, not directly from their step-parents, while adopted children inherit in the same way as biological children, since they have the same legal status. Children born outside marriage inherit equally from their father in the same way as other children. Heirs can only claim two-thirds of parents' estates, with the other third available for distribution in any will or testament. However, within that two-thirds, the general presumption is that each sibling should inherit equally, and where a will is not present, the law prescribes that heirs should receive equal parts of the estate.

Partible inheritance through family branches potentially implies an ever-expanding number of owners through the generations. When property is distributed equally (e.g. when a person dies intestate), part ownership of a cabin may be left in equal shares to all siblings. Each sibling may then divide their part shares to leave to their own children, the number of heirs thus rising exponentially. Within only two or three generations, the

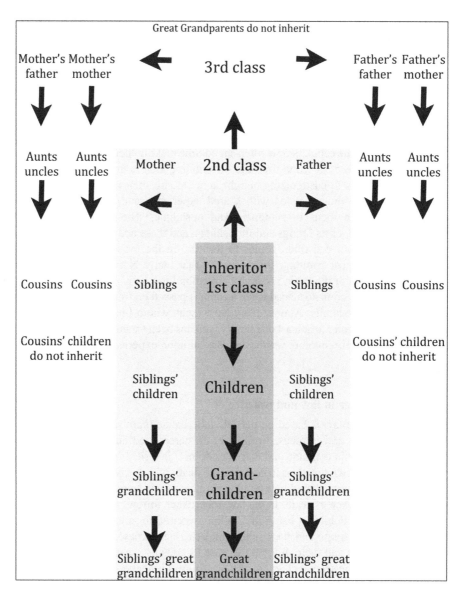

Figure 1.   Inheritance table (after Lødrup 1999).

number of part owners may be large, and historically this has been the fate of older cabins. Some of these part owners may already be second-generation emigrants, typically in America, or perhaps Australia, and be quite unknown to the remaining relations in Norway. In some cases, annual get-togethers to work on the cabin can be an opportunity to reinstate distant kin relationships, and it may indeed be the only occasion on which kin meet. However, cabins require maintenance and hence investment, and it may be the case that decisions cannot be taken on these matters, and certainly not on the question of sale, without all owners giving permission, which can, in time, lead to the ruin of a cabin. One remedy that some co-owners have taken is to set up a kind of share recall, whereby owners are offered a limited time to sell or buy each other's shares in the property, and a new co-ownership contract may be established, for example, with a fixed number of shares that cannot then be further divided on inheritance.

What this highlights is also the possibility of adapting inheritance law in practice, through the drawing up of a will, on the one hand, but also by establishing contracts of sale of various kinds that preempt the will and allow owners to adapt inheritance laws in practice. In other words, inheritance law is one thing, but inheritance practices are another, and although practices may be based in law, or may use the law, they also provide a form of interpretation of the law and the continuation of commonplace ideas about what the law should offer, as I will return to below.

Within a co-ownership contract, ownership may be inherited through different branches of a family leading to variation between share ownerships. For instance, Siblings A, B and C inherit a third share each in a cabin left to them by their parents. Sibling A divides their share between their three children, who thus each inherit a ninth through their branch of the family. B's two children each inherit a sixth, and C dies without surviving children, so his third is divided into 5 and is distributed through the other branches, with each of the other heirs getting an additional fifteenth share from C. A's children then own 8/45, and B's own 7/30 (Figure 2). In family O, for example, a property is shared between relatives as follows: Katrin owns 2/72, Bart and Kjersti own 1/72 each, Isold and Rikard own 22/72 each, while Tor owns 24/72. What we see is a kind of mathematics of kinship played out through the inheritance of shares in a cabin, and complex calculations in this kinship maths need to be reckoned at the point of inheritance.

In practice, there are many ways to organize the division of property on inheritance. It is common for the inheritance of cabins to be organized once a family's children become adults, or as parents reach retirement. There are some tax benefits to handing over property in life, but it is also a means to ensure that any potential conflicts inspired by the inheritance are dealt with by the parents, rather than leaving siblings to fall out after they die. Family R provides one such example:

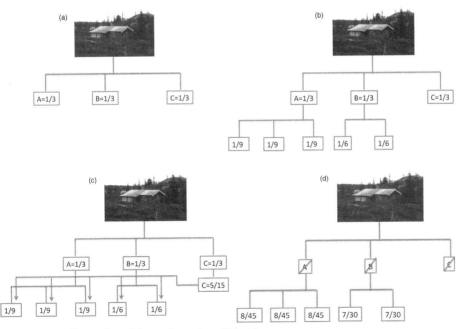

Figure 2.   An illustration of the mathematics of kinship.

Mr and Mrs R own a third share in a cabin, whose other two-thirds are owned by Mr R's brothers. Mr R is elderly and in poor health, and wishes to organize his will. He decides that in dividing his property between his three children, his daughter will inherit his 1/3 share in the cabin, but he wishes to offer his two sons the right to first refusal if his daughter decides to sell her share. For this, he will seek the approval of his brothers. Mr and Mrs R retain the right to use the cabin for four weeks each year (the maximum allowable before the tax authorities consider it not to have changed ownership), specifying two particular weeks in July, and two others to be arranged ad hoc each year. The daughter thus takes over a third share in the cabin, her parents retain four weeks use per year and the sons have the right to purchase the cabin if the daughter decides to sell. The third share implies a continued negotiation with the other two owners, the father's siblings, who may in turn leave their shares to their own children. In consequence, the daughter must remain in regular contact with her uncles and aunts to negotiate cabin use and maintenance, and she would be wise to consult her brothers if she has thoughts about selling up.

The first-buyer right is widespread in Norway and seems to be derived from the principle of 'Odel'. Odel law (Landbruks- og Matdepartementet, 1974) derives from Norrøn law and was intended to keep farms in the family rather than being divided up into uneconomic fractions through partible inheritance, in other words precisely to avoid the problems outlined earlier in this paper. An oldest son had the Odel right to inherit his father's farm, and if it was sold out of the family, he retained the right to buy it back within a number of years. The association between farm and family overrode other rights, such as a buyer's property rights, reflecting the degree of significance given to a family's ownership of land and property, which in turn were central to issues of identity, name and belonging. Odel, or Allodial Rights continue to operate in relation to farming and forestry land over a certain size (25 hectares of farmed land, 500 hectares of forest, Odelsloven §2), and allodial rights can be valid up to two years after a sale (§ 20b). Odel does not apply to cabins, generally speaking, although the principle of priority of purchase is often written into contracts to try to keep cabins in a family. This may be included alongside the equal distribution of property through inheritance. So although Odel law does not apply, the principle of keeping property whole, and/ or keeping it in the family, remains a popular and significant principle, and Odel law is mimicked through the drawing up of contracts that entail rights of purchase, first refusal for offers of sale or rights to demand shares in ownership during property transactions. Rights of first refusal, on the other hand, are governed by a set of legal principles covered by '*Loysningsrettar*'[4] (of which Odel is one particular instance), which allows for a set of rights to first refusal, ranging from the right to purchase before a property goes onto the open market, to the right to purchase from the buyer at the market price.

In general terms, equality between siblings remains an overriding principle in Norwegian inheritance law and in common practice (for a critique of Norwegian equality generally: see Lien, Lidén, & Vike, 2001). In order to inherit equally, property must be divided, and this may be done by distributing items of equal value, by sharing ownership of them (and the obligations and costs this entails), or by attributing a monetary value to all items and dividing them accordingly. Where more than one property of different financial values is to be divided, siblings may thus be able to inherit a single property, but be compensated financially for the difference in value between the different properties. A particular cause of dispute and resentment arises where siblings have different desires in relation to this property. In principle, one sibling may buy out the others, thereby compensating them financially for their share. In R's case, the daughter's siblings are compensated through inheriting other property owned by the parents, but the parents take steps to retain the cabin in the family by giving first-buyer rights to the sons. Keeping the cabin in the family is often a primary consideration when cabins are to be inherited. However, in other cases, one sibling may either not wish to retain a share in the cabin, for various reasons. These may include personal preference, or the desire to liquidate the value of the property to use for other purposes. In this case, the sibling (or part owner) can effectively put their share up for sale, with or without the agreement of the other owners (see below).

'Modern families'

In practice, a couple may own a primary residence, and one or more cabins. If the number of cabins is equal to the number of children, parents may decide to leave one to each, perhaps according to their degree of attachment to the different places. They may equally decide to instruct their offspring to share a cabin and enter into a co-ownership arrangement. Co-ownership may entail a formal contract that specifies how the co-ownership is to be managed, what rights are distributed, what obligations are shared, which weeks respective owners may use the cabin or what degree of autonomy they have over maintenance or renovation.

Things get a little more complicated when contemporary family structures are taken into consideration. Couples who have 'her children, his children and our children', that is, who bring children into a marriage and then have further children together, may have a more complex relation to the division of property. While property jointly owned may be left equally to all the children, property brought into the marriage may be retained under 'particular ownership', that is, held outside the marriage. Such property must be registered as '*særeie*', and will then be inherited only by the direct offspring of the partner owning the property, and not their step-children. This quite often relates to cabins, which one partner may inherit from their own parents, and wishes to keep within that family branch. The branches indicated in the illustration above (Figure 1) reflect a commonly held set of assumptions about kinship and the 'naturalness' of property flowing along the lines of biological (or adoptive) generational kin relations. This can be disputed, though, and forms another moment of tension in the route of property through kinship (or kinship through property).

For example, family Risdal's cabin appeared in a court case reported in Agder high court in February 2012. Olav Risdal bought a cabin at auction for his teenaged son, Roald, in 1971. In 1982, Roald sold the cabin back to his father for 50,000 kroner, under condition that he retained the right to purchase it back at the same price if the property were to be sold or at the point of inheritance. When Olav, and then his wife Anne died, Roald claimed the right to repurchase the cabin. But Anne had two children from an earlier marriage, and left three heirs, a son Arne, and two grandchildren, Olav and Diana, the children of the second, deceased son. Arne, Olav and Diana disputed Roald's claim to the cabin and argued that since it was not held outside the marriage, it formed part of the general estate and that they should thus retain rights to inherit. Without going into the details of the case and its resolution, it indicates that the rights of step-siblings are disputable, while the rights of siblings are less easily challenged. One can only speculate at this point what the effect of taking this case to the high court may have on the relationship between the siblings, nieces and nephews, but it appears unlikely that the cabin will fulfill its idealized role in the future as a place where the extended family gather to share their holidays. In this case, the cabin has a kind of contradictory role, where from one direction it kins the step-siblings through their argument that they are equally beneficiaries of the marriage and its shared property, while from the other side, it de-kins the step-siblings by asserting the primacy of the father–son relation in this buying of the cabin specifically for the son, and the maintenance of this prioritization through the specifying of a subsequent first-repurchase right for the son.

The issue at stake in the Risdal case appears to have been the price that Roald should pay for the cabin into the estate of his late parents before it was distributed between the heirs. While the sum paid to Roald by his father was a nominal sum, his co-heirs wanted him to pay the market value to purchase the property. While sales between family members do not necessarily correspond with market values, if the sale is arranged after the owner dies intestate, the legal norm for disbursing an estate requires the executors of the will to appoint an expert advisor to set a reasonable market value on the property, to be used to calculate both death taxes and the shares distributed to the heirs. While the market value of modest mountain cabins in less fashionable areas may mirror inflation, cabins in popular areas have changed in value quite radically in the past half-century. A small seaside cabin along the Oslo fjord that may have been built by or for a married couple in the 1950s or 1960s for a few thousand Norwegian kroner may now be worth several million kroner (hundreds of thousands, or even millions of Euros). If one of a group of heirs does not wish to participate in a co-ownership contract, for whatever reason, the others are obliged to buy them out, but if they do not have several million kroner available to buy the share of the exiting heir, they may be forced to go onto the open market to sell the dearly beloved cabin of their parents, where they have spent so many happy childhood summer holidays, and where they have always met to spend a few summer days together as a family ever since. Silje, for example, returned to Norway newly married in the 1980s after several years studying abroad, when her older sister decided she wanted to sell her share in their inherited summer cabin on the fjord a couple of hours drive south of Oslo to buy something she preferred for her own family. Silje had no means of raising the substantial capital she would have needed to buy her sister's share and was forced to see the cabin sold off. While she gained enough financially to help her buy a property in Oslo, she regrets even now the loss of the cabin. Its market value has risen so much that she would never be able to purchase it back, even as a well-established and generously paid professional. So while the benefit of financial compensation through the sale of the property may provide some solace, the loss of the emotional tie, the possibility of returning to the cabin for future holidays, can be a major loss, and one that exacerbates the bereavement that has brought about the sale, and in some cases may cause a long-lasting family rift and years of extended grief or bitterness.

A similar outcome may result from the lack of long-term financial planning of owners, if the cabin is subject to inheritance tax that may be unaffordable for those who inherit the property, since the inheritance tax is calculated in relation to market value, not the value of a property when constructed and subject to normal inflation. A cabin may thus be sold out of the family on inheritance, simply because the heirs cannot afford to pay the tax that accrues on a modest property that has become caught up in a wild property bubble. Again, the cabin may be lost to the family, and with it the occasion of negotiating over the use of the cabin, the possibility of meeting there for holidays and special occasions, and sharing of the care of the cabin itself that the property demands. As the cabin moves out of joint, or family ownership, the family itself is reduced by the shared demands that co-ownership of property entails. One could argue that the practice of kinship is reduced in this way, in proportion to the extent that kinship is enhanced by the sharing of ownership and care for a cabin.

Legal advice and legal roles

Many of the problems outlined above are well known. Where cabin owners are concerned to avoid such difficulties, they may well consult a solicitor for advice about inheritance and tax planning. There are solicitors who specialize in such issues, but most inheritance specialists will have a good knowledge of cabin-specific issues. What is more, interviews with such professionals indicate that they may also have strong opinions on the form that such inheritance should take. That is, despite strong protestations that all Cabin cases are different, solicitors in particular may have strong moral views on the correct form of inheritance, driven in particular by experience of the legal wrangles that often arise from disputes between the beneficiaries of inheritance. Interviews indicate that solicitors often recommend against co-ownership, since it can lead to disputes among co-owners. One solicitor, very experienced in inheritance issues, explained his skepticism to co-ownership through reference to time and further inheritance:

> it can go very well for the first generation, but then it goes to cousins and becomes a bit distant, then it gets even more distant, some will use it more than others, and some will do more of the maintenance and there are different interests. From being a lovely opportunity to meet up, it becomes a point of conflict, where people fall out with each other.

Some people manage it, he acknowledged, but in his view, it depends largely on their personalities as well as the kind of management regime that has been put in place, a view echoed by other solicitors in interviews. Another solicitor recounted that when his parents became too elderly to maintain a sweet little cabin by the sea, he proposed to his siblings that they draw lots to see who would inherit it. The summer season is short and cabins require maintenance, so it would barely be worth sharing the cabin. Although it was difficult (emotionally) to draw lots for the cabin, it was a simple solution. The losers of the lottery would inherit a share in the parents' house in Oslo – which, since each of them already had a house, was later sold. As he explained, people put a great deal of love into their cabins.[5]

Despite their reluctance, a legal system does exist that allows for co-ownership, in contrast to the British system (which requires ownership by more than two persons to be owned through a Trust). Norwegian law allows for shared ownership between spouses, or through the law on joint ownership. The latter, 'Sameieloven',[6] allows for unequal ownership between parties (i.e. one can own 70% and another 30%) and allows parties to a joint ownership to leave the arrangement at any time and without any particular reason; this is what is called a declaratory law, one that allows for arrangements that are outside or beyond the arrangements specified in the law (i.e. particular contracts can have their own clauses). Joint ownership may be one means of sharing a cabin, but is only one part of the law that is brought into play in the inheritance of cabins, and the variation possible within the law allows for many different specific agreements. As one solicitor outlined, clauses may detail everything from who brings in the firewood, to who will use the cabin at Easter, as well as details about who may purchase a share from who and in what circumstances. Often when these arrangements are to be put in place, or when a contract or a will has not been drawn up, people come to solicitors to help sort out the inheritance and deal with the tax arrangements.

Given this central role of legal professionals in the inheritance of cabins, it is perhaps surprising that so little attention has been given by social scientists and particularly by anthropologists to the role of legal practices at critical moments for kinship. In this context, legal professionals have a significant role in not only translating the wishes of their clients into legal documentation, but also in persuading them how they should formalize their desires for the future of their family, via the distribution of ownership of their property. A highly experienced solicitor suggests, for example, that as I see it, in principle, parents decide to organize things in advance, since that way their children can fall out with them, but that is less of a disaster than that they should argue between themselves for the rest of their lives.

Instead, a system of compensation through monetary value can be brought into play to resolve any potential inequalities, or at least to help to salve any potential hurt. This particular solicitor strongly urged clients not to simply allow their children to share property, but to allocate one property to one child, and give money to the others – better, in his view, to allow one offspring to buy out the others and own a lovely big cabin unshared.

On the other hand, when such arrangements are not put in place, it is often shortly after a death that a family appears at the solicitor's office to deal with the inheritance, at which point disagreements often materialize. The solicitor may thus end up practicing a form of pastoral care in helping the family to resolve the tensions that are collecting around property ownership. In a sense, the solicitor also acts in a pastoral sense when advising clients on their forward inheritance practices. As mentioned above, making arrangements in advance to transfer ownership of a cabin, while retaining some use-rights (and allocating use-rights to other members of the family) is common, but is not legally a will. Such transfers are generally done as a form of purchase contracts, or what might be known in English as conveyance. While the legal niceties are not crucial here, two things are clear. Firstly, kinship is performed in a particular way through the transfer of ownership of a cabin, and secondly, the law and legal professionals have a key role in smoothing the way of this potentially difficult moment of re-defining kin relations, and in shaping those relations through particular forms of the distribution and disbursement of property.

Conclusions

It is clear from the above discussion that market values intrude on the sentimental and affective values of the cabin in key ways. Market value can become a contested quantity in the settlement of distributive inheritance, and it may become a barrier to the maintenance of ownership of the cabin among heirs where the market value soars above their financial means. Market or cash value is generally seen as opposed to the sentimental value historically invested in the cabin through the practice of families going to and being at the cabin together, such that one might see them as two regimes of value coming into conflict. The heavy emphasis given to enjoying family life together at the cabin, and the focus of leisure and pleasure at the cabin serve to emphasize the kinship of the cabin itself. The cabin is where the family gathers, it requires care from the family (maintenance) and provides a reason for family to indulge in joint activities (skiing, hiking, food gathering, playing games, eating and drinking together, etc.) becoming, one could argue, a member of that family in its own way.

But the point of this paper is that cabins are enmeshed in a far wider range of value regimes than might be assumed from tax statements and asset declarations. Not only do they have affective value for those who have spent time at the cabin, but they have a role in a quite different regime of value, in gathering, conjoining, distinguishing and dividing kin. Shared inherited ownership becomes a means to prolong siblingship relations beyond the life of parents, and thus a means of securing at least first cousin (grandchildren), if not further generations of (great-grandchildren, etc.) kinship relations. Cabins also signify family togetherness, and are substantially used to effect family closeness (see Abram, 2012), and thus the imperative of keeping the cabin in the family can be understood as a desire to keep the family together. Closer study of the details of cabin-kinship also reveals otherwise underemphasized details in kinship reproduction, namely the creation of a distinction between half-siblings, who inherit separately from their legal (i.e. biological or adoptive) siblings, and step-parents. At the same time, we should remember Appadurai's concern that the idea of a regime of value is to suggest that as items are exchanged (in this case through inheritance or through the market), the degree of cultural sharing of values may indeed be variable. While some families make extraordinary efforts to ensure that they use the cabin to secure siblingship (e.g. Aasheim & Nordby, 2011), others insist that co-ownership is sure to result in family quarrels. Little research is currently available on the practices of foreign owners of Norwegian cabins (of whom there appear to be growing numbers), while alpine skiing apartments are increasingly taking the place of cabins among downhill skiing enthusiasts, and it is not yet clear whether these fit into the general cabin model. Implicit in the whole of this discussion is also the question of nationalism, since what is under consideration here is 'Norwegian' cabins. Certainly, similarities with Swedish, Danish or Finnish cabin practices may be identified, but many practices associated with Norwegian cabins, and practiced under Norwegian law, are also implicated in the generation of a sense of Norwegianness (see Ween & Abram, 2012). There are certainly variations in the extent to which cabins are seen as commodities rather than heritage, and in the kinds of cabin that are more marketable quantities subject to urban styling, rather than simple holiday dwellings. By tracing some of the arrangements made for the inheritance of cabins, the outlines of these regimes of value should become clearer.

What I have shown in this paper is that holiday homes are not just places to have a holiday. Economic, environmental and social impacts of holiday homes are well recognized, but cabins may also reveal to us a great deal about the significance of ownership, and in turn of kinship and all that that entails. Economic impact is not only felt in terms of 'spend', but in the sharing of assets within and between families, and in the obligations that owners have towards their cabins and thus to each other. It helps us to understand why people travel to particular places, how they choose when to visit, who to invite, what to bring and what to do there. It also shows us that 'value' is a highly contested quality.

Notes

1. A contested term, since it presumes one residence is 'primary' which is very often not the case. Use of the term here should be read as though within quotation marks.
2. In what has been referred to as 'prosumption' (Toffler, 1980).
3. Thanks to Ingun Grimstad Klepp for this observation.
4. *Lov om løysingsrettar.* Justis- og beredskapsdepartementet LOV-1994-12-09-64.
5. '*noe som folk har spesielt lagt elsk på*'.
6. Lov om sameige [sameigelova]. Justis- og beredskapsdepartementet. LOV-1965-06-18-6.

References

Aasheim, A., & Nordby, C. M. (2011, July 15). Idyll på Deling: Forfall er det første tegnet på at noe erg alt. Én av fem krangler om hytta. *A-magasinet*, pp. 20–25.

Abram, S. (2012). The normal cabin's revenge: Building Norwegian (holiday) home-cultures. *Home Cultures*, 9(3), 233–255.

Appadurai, A. (1986). Commodities and the politics of value. In A. Appadurai (Ed.), *The social life of things* (pp. 3–63). Cambridge: Cambridge University Press.

Bloch, M. (2004). The resurrection of the house amongst the Zafimaniry of Madagascar. In J. Carsten & S. Hugh-Jones (Eds.), *About the house: Levi-Strauss and beyond* (pp. 69–83). Cambridge: Cambridge University Press.

Carsten, J., & Hugh-Jones, S. (2004). Introduction: About the house – Levi-Strauss and beyond. In J. Carsten & S. Hugh-Jones (Eds.), *About the house: Levi-Strauss and beyond* (pp. 1–46). Cambridge: Cambridge University Press.

Dalsgaard, S. (2013). The commensurability of carbon: Making value and money of climate change. *HAU: Journal of Ethnographic Theory, 3*(1), 80–98.

Flognfeldt, T., Jr. (2004). Second homes as a part of a new rural lifestyle in Norway. In M. Hall & D. Müller (Eds.), *Tourism, mobility and second homes* (pp. 233–43). Clevedon: Channel View.

Gallent, N., & Tewdwr-Jones, M. (2000). *Rural second homes in Europe: Housing supply and planning control*. Aldershot: Ashgate.

Hall, C. M., & Müller, D. K. (2004). *Tourism, mobility and second homes: Between elite landscape and common ground*. Clevedon: Channel View.

Howell, S. (2006). *Kinning of foreigners: Transnational adoption in a global perspective*. Oxford: Berghahn Books.

Kaltenborn, B. P. (1998). The alternate home – motives of recreation home use. *Norsk Geografisk Tidsskrift – Norwegian Journal of Geography, 52*, 121–134.

Landbruks- og Matdepartementet. (1974). *LOV 1974–06–28 nr 58: Lov om odelsretten og åsetesretten* [odelslova]. Oslo: Lovdata.

Lien, M., Lidén, H., & Vike, H. (2001). *Likhetens paradokser: antropologiske undersøkelser i det moderne Norge*. Oslo: Universitetsforlaget.

Lødrup, P. (1999). Arverett (4. utg.). Oslo: P. Lødrup. Retrieved from http://www.nb.no/nbsok/nb/e2489674c57412e9f25142b6bc0fd7e6.nbdigital?lang=no

Malinowski, B. (1922). *Argonauts of the Western Pacific*. London: George Routledge & Sons, Ltd.

Meek, J. (2014). Where will we live? *London Review of Books, 36*(1), 7–16.

Munn, N. D. (1986). *The fame of Gawa: A symbolic study of value transformation in a Massim (Papua New Guinea) society*. Cambridge: Cambridge University Press.

Ortiz, H. (2013). Financial value: Economic, moral, political, global. *HAU: Journal of Ethnographic Theory, 3*(1), 64–79.

Otto, T., & Willerslev, R. (2013). Introduction: 'Value as theory' comparison, cultural critique, and guerilla ethnographic theory. *HAU: Journal of Ethnographic Theory, 3*(1), 1–20.

Strang, V., & Busse, M. (Eds.). (2011). *Ownership and appropriation*. Oxford: Berg.

Strathern, M. (2011). Sharing, stealing and borrowing simultaneously. In V. Strang & M. Busse (Eds.), *Ownership and appropriation* (pp. 23–42). Oxford: Berg.

Toffler, A. (1980). *The third wave*. London: Collins.

Tsing, A. (2013). Sorting out commodities how capitalist value is made through gifts. *HAU: Journal of Ethnographic Theory, 3*(1), 21–43.

Ween, G., & Abram, S. (2012). The Norwegian trekking association: Trekking as constituting the nation. *Landscape Research, 37*(2), 155–171.

Weiner, A. B. (1976). *Women of value, men of renown: New perspectives in Trobriand exchange*. Austin: University of Texas Press.

Value of silence: mediating aural environments in Estonian rural tourism

Maarja Kaaristo

Department of Ethnology, Institute for Cultural Studies and Fine Arts, University of Tartu, Ülikooli, Estonia

This paper concentrates on the creation of value(s) by rural tourism entrepreneurs via intangible and atmospheric natural resources, the aural environment. The creation of value is analysed with regard to how the rural tourism entrepreneurs facilitate and mediate the aural environment of their farms to their guests and how by doing so the notions of rurality and rural environment are constantly (re)created and (re)negotiated. The paper concentrates on the notion of 'silence' which the tourism farmers regard as one of the most valuable qualities of their environments and shows how the personal experience of the host is one of the most important aspects when creating and mediating the experience for the visitors. The paper begins with a theoretic discussion of the idea of rural idyll, after which the research background is described with a brief overview of the Estonian rural context and the description of the methodology and empirical data of the article. This is followed by the analysis of the gathered data which is divided into two main topics: the creation of value by the tourism entrepreneurs when constructing the rural sound idyll and the question of competing values in the rural tourism context.

Introduction

Tourism is a phenomenon that encompasses a complicated mixture of human emotions, fears and desires, backgrounds, inclinations, choices and values. It is fashioned by politics, power, current consumer styles, the travel industry and the tourist herself (Edensor, 2006). Travel involves some kind of physical movement from one place to another and, when we mentally (re)construct our environments and the meanings we give to travel, we often rely on our personal (or collective) values in order to choose the (next) destination. Similarly, hosts also rely on their sets of values when welcoming tourists, offering their visitors what they feel the visitors consider important and creating environments that they hope will be enjoyed and appreciated.

'Rural tourism is tourism that takes place in the countryside' as put rather straightfor-wardly by Lane (2012, p. 355). Of course, defining 'rural' and 'countryside' is a challenge; it has been noted (Hoggart, 1990, p. 245) that stressing the rural–urban dichotomy is not a very fruitful approach and that the similarities of rural and urban have not received enough attention. Generally speaking, the rural is rather a social construct, 'an imagined entity that is brought into being by particular discourses of rurality that are produced, reproduced and contested' by very different stakeholders (Woods, 2011, p. 9) and some views of rurality as exemplified on the issue of aural environments will be discussed in this paper. Modifying activities by the humans, such as clearing woodlands to plant crops, etc. have created a rural landscape, a *countryside*, that is neither wild nor urban, and that is quite often appreciated for its picturesque scenery in public discourses (Farrell & Russell, 2011, p. 100). Rural tourism can be viewed as a phenomenon resulting partly from the wish to escape the urban environment and the need to reaffirm personal identities in the face of growing urban-isation. However, we should not necessarily see it only as a 'kind of retreat from complex-ity, into the half-remembered vistas of familiarity and simplicity associated with the past' (Dicks, 2003, p. 130), as rural tourism is a multifaceted phenomenon where very different actors and stakeholders, needs, interests and desires form complex webs of meanings and regimes of value.

Drawing on my fieldwork on Estonian rural tourism establishments, I will explore some notions of how contemporary rural entrepreneurs see and interpret their environments, what they consider important and how they understand their guests' wishes and visions of the rural. I will concentrate on the notion and value of 'silence' or 'peace and quiet': the specific rural aural environment that tourism farmers regard as one of the most important qualities of their surroundings. I will discuss how tourism farmers facilitate and mediate this aural environment (the rural sound idyll) to their guests and how, by doing so, they constantly (re)create and (re)negotiate the notion of rurality. I will look at the construction and creation of value by tourism farmers through intangible and atmospheric natural resources, such as the auditory environment and the sense of peace found – or at least offered – in the studied farms.

The rural idyll: Arcadia for the hosts and guests

A modified rural environment, with traditional-style farmhouses, domesticated animals, fields, lakes, ponds, etc. ('the rural idyll'), can be viewed as a certain 'trope', a symbol of rurality and the (peasant) past, just as Urry (2002 [1990], p. 128) describes an aspect of the *tourist gaze*, where one learns that 'a thatched cottage with roses round the door rep-resents "ye olde England"'. Following from this, a wooden country house surrounded by a forest and fields, with a garden of apple trees in a relatively secluded area, preferably near a pond or lake and definitely with a sauna, is a marker of 'real' rural southern Estonia, an image harnessed by tourism farm owners in a variety of manners. Nugin (2014, pp. 57–58) identifies the rural idyll constructed in Estonian public media discourse as depicting rural inhabitants as 'courageous, durable, hard-working, shrewd and clever' people who do not complain about the hardships of rural life (such as demanding farm work, extreme weather conditions, etc.) and live in harmonious communities helping each other out and working towards common goals. The creation and interpretation of rural environments is very individual. These 'tropes' are formed in the interaction of each individ-ual's values and personal reading of certain signs and markers, the questions of authority that lie in the gazes of both hosts and the guests upon particular sites, as well as the power dynamics of managing those representations and experiences.

Abram (2003) expands on Urry's concept of the tourist gaze in rural settings, introdu-cing the idea of the *rural gaze* and, in line with Veijola and Jokinen (1994), stresses the need 'to reconnect the seeing-eye to the rest of the body' (Abram, 2003, p. 34). Visual perception is definitely not the only way to consume the (rural) environment, as has been noted by Soile Veijola and Eeva Jokinen in their above-mentioned seminal article 'The Body in Tourism' (1994), where they show that all human senses are engaged when 'doing tourism' (an expression used by Crouch (1999), who stresses the proactive, participatory and processual nature of leisure) and, depending on the particular experience and occasion, different senses may be engaged. The surrounding environment is comprehensive visual and experiential phenomenon which is created in the people's minds via sensory observations (Tuohino & Pitkänen, 2004, p. 79) and the rural gaze is experienced in an embodied way though a complex maze of senses – sounds, smells, vision, taste and touch – as well as through social organisation and experience. It directs and manages the ways different phenomena are seen, and also 'what is deemed appropriate to be seen, and motivates people to change the appearance of the land to conform with their ideals' (Abram, 2003, p. 40). Therefore, the rural gaze is political and value-laden and can be seen as resulting from negotiations between different parties.

The rural can be perceived, created and consumed as something nostalgic, although this nostalgia does not mean seeking the 'actual past', but rather

> a sanitised, picturesque vision, where old houses are renovated to contain modern conveniences, and are spruced up well beyond the state they would have been in when new. This gaze, in other words, is not referential only to the past, but seeks an improved, idealised (and some would say suburban or modern) vision'.[1] (Abram, 2003, p. 44)

This is an imagined rural space that van Koppen (2000, pp. 303–307) calls Arcadia,[2] where people live in harmony with nature, appreciating its beauty and placing high value on it in emotional, moral and aesthetic ways. In the case of Estonian rural tourism, this is usually 'backed up' by modern amenities (such as wireless internet), should the guest wish to revert to their urbanite ways. A modern idyllic countryside, where one can indulge in various forms of nostalgia (longing for paradise, the simple life, past times, and the return to childhood, as typified by Dann (1994)), is thus not a retreat from the present to the past but rather an ongoing process stimulated by it (Dicks, 2003, p. 131).

Researching Estonian tourism farms

Family farming had been an important source of livelihood in Estonia, with its mainly agricultural economy, up until the 1940s. In 1944, most of the land was collectivised and previous farms became small households, 'plot farms', where people could grow vegetables and raise farm animals for their personal needs. After Estonia regained its independence in 1991, the agricultural system was reorganised by closing the collective farms and through the privatisation process, where the owners of property in 1940 or their heirs could apply for restitution of the land that had belonged to them before its appropriation by the state during the Soviet period. In principle, this gave these landowners an opportunity to take up small-scale farming, but in reality this was extremely hard to do due to Estonia's agricultural policies. Most of the farm owners quit farming quickly, since it was unprofitable (Grubbström & Sooväli-Sepping, 2012, pp. 330–331). Several of the interviewed tourism farmers had tried farming at some point in the early 1990s, but all except for one farm had given up due to changed conditions: when the big meat and dairy manufacturers stopped buying meat and milk from small producers (for a brief overview of the transition period of the 1990s in rural areas and the contemporary rural situation in Estonia, see Nugin, 2014, pp. 53–54).

The collapse of the Soviet Union in 1991 was also an important factor that allowed for the development of Estonian rural tourism on a larger and more international scale. Before that, tourism was regulated by the state and therefore there were no small-scale rural tourism entrepreneurs. It has to be noted, however, that many entrepreneurs did start their activities as early as the 1970s and 1980s (even though it was not supported by the state legislation). In 1992, the Department of Tourism was created at the Estonian Farmers' Central Union in order to help its members find additional sources of income besides their agricultural production (Ardel, 2004, p. 44) and one of the alternatives to the traditional production farm was to become a farm for the tourists.[3] This transition, in a wider European context, has been described by Busby and Rendle (2000), who showed how the emphasis changed from 'tourism on a farm' to 'farm tourism', where the component relating to tourism became the main activity of many farm businesses, replacing 'traditional' farm life.

The fieldwork for this paper was conducted in Võru County, in south-east Estonia. Southern Estonia is one of the most popular rural tourism destinations in Estonia, along with western Estonia and the islands. The area mostly advertises its nature tourism (hiking, canoeing, wild berry and mushroom picking and fishing) and culture tourism (the local Võro dialect,[4] the tradition of playing the local variety of the concertina, the *Teppo lõõts*, food, and the culture of the *Setos*, the latter being under the protection of UNESCO intangible cultural heritage and has therefore gathered quite a lot of media attention in recent years[5]).

During the first field trip in 2008, I mainly studied issues related to local identity but, after my attention was shifted to the general topic of tourism by my colleague Ester Bardone (then Võsu), we undertook a second field trip to study issues mainly related to rural tourism (Võsu & Kaaristo, 2009). Although initially our questionnaire did not include questions about the aural environment, I began to focus on the issue while analysing the responses to the interviews conducted in 2008, in which the farmers quite often talked about the acoustic elements of their surroundings and the importance they placed on them in their lives. The preliminary discussion of what the farmers perceived as 'silence' and its close connection to rural temporalities can be found in Kaaristo and Järv (2012, pp. 125–128).

I visited 11 different tourism farms in short 'back-and-forth' field trips and conducted altogether 13 in-depth interviews between 2008 and 2013. All the interviews except for two were conducted at the entrepreneurs' respective farms. Two couples were interviewed together; ten interviews were conducted by me and Ester Bardone, and three by me. All the interviews (except for one unstructured interview in 2013) were semi-structured lasting from an hour to two and a half hours. The questionnaire concentrated on the following topics: the farmers' general opinions about tourism in Võru County and in Estonia, the farm owners' motivation for going into the hospitality business, their guests and different services provided at the farms, local life in general, also local culture and environment with regard to the tourism and hospitality services. The interviews (conducted in Estonian, all fully transcribed and then thematically analysed), the field diaries (sound diary, and the fieldwork diaries describing the (participant) observation and the interview situations), photos, informal conversations with both the entrepreneurs and local people, and, to a smaller extent, the web pages of tourism farms, comprise the empirical source material of this paper.

In 2013, I specifically paid attention to the aural, sound and acoustic elements in tourism farmers' narrations during interviews when in the field and I started keeping a sound diary in addition to my regular fieldwork diary. It was not easy to study sound, which 'inhabits its own time and dissipates quickly' and is 'too brief and ephemeral to attract much attention, let alone occupy the tangible duration favoured by methods of research' (Kahn, 1999, p. 5). I engaged in 'deep listening' (Bull & Back, 2003, p. 4) of my surroundings when in the field, an alert, thoughtful and critical type of auditory attention, with the intention of comprehending how the world surrounding us becomes present through the variety of its sounds.

Creating value: the rural sound idyll

Values (as opinions and principles belonging to people) are 'ends, goals, interests, beliefs, ethics, biases, attitudes, traditions, morals and objectives that change with human perception and with time' (Henning, 1974, p. 15). People lean on their values when making choices and decisions in the course of their lives that make actions meaningful. The social psychologists Bilsky and Schwartz (1994) see these personal values as cognitive representations of people's needs, which comprise beliefs or behaviours, and which guide our choices and the ways we assess different situations and experiences. The phenomenon of tourism is simultaneously an expression and experience of such values, its practices emerging from the normative cultural environment surrounding us (Jamal & Robinson, 2012, p. 3).

However, the idea of value can also be looked at as a property belonging to various commodities; according to Arjun Appadurai

> value is embodied in commodities that are exchanged. Focusing on things that are exchanged, rather than simply on the forms or functions of exchange, makes it possible to argue that what creates the link between exchange and value is *politics,* constructed broadly. (1986, p. 3, original italics)

Therefore, various material and immaterial objects and phenomena obtain value (be it emotional, aesthetic or spiritual) in the eyes of individuals and social groups – and the value as a belief about something can thus be transformed into value as property. The hosts' and guests' values that are reverberated in the appreciation of certain rural environments can at some point be transformed into the economic, monetary value attached to an overnight stay at rural tourism enterprise for example. But value is also embodied in the intangible 'commodities' traded between rural tourism hosts and guests – intangible natural or atmospheric phenomena, just like people and commodities, also have social lives. So, rural tourism can be seen as an arena where different values meet and have to be negotiated between different agents and where the value-as-belief is transformed into value-as-property and back again, creating various 'regimes of value' (Appadurai, 1986). The rural environments themselves do not have an 'intrinsic value or meaning: these are established and re-established continually' (Tacchi, 2012 [1998], p. 26) in each specific environment.

In tourism research, values as cognitive representations have mostly been studied in understanding that people's beliefs and end goals are important keys to understanding tourist motivation. According to Weeden (2011), who used Schwartz's value survey to determine the values underpinning the choices of responsible tourists, the tourists claimed to have found a sense of 'inner peace' by being close to nature, giving up modern consumption demands and achieving a sense of renewal from experiencing the surrounding nature. Indeed, as Kaplan (1984, p. 190) has suggested, natural surroundings are often 'proclaimed for their capacity to instil a sense of peace and serenity. ... Somehow, tranquillity is more readily achieved in the natural context'. The tourism farmers of Võru County recognise the potential commercial and economical values of their environment that lie in these types of beliefs and needs. Thus, the 'tourist efforts to consume culture are incorporated into local cultural systems of meaning and transformed according to local values' (Annist, 2013, p. 253) when hosts and guests interact.

Sensory perception in general and auditory experience in particular are simultaneously social, cultural and physical commodities; in addition to reacting to or perceiving physical phenomena, our senses also channel our personal values. In rural tourism, as evident from my fieldwork, the values-as-beliefs of the hosts are very important and can shape and influence the tourism establishment in significant ways. It is often the case that tourism farmers share these values with their guests or at least that is what is hoped for; the tourism farmers expect that the perceived tranquillity of their surroundings is appreciated by their guests. The personal values that guide both hosts and guests are determining factors that help to shape an aural environment that is suitable for both the giving and the receiving ends of these tourism situations and, in this interaction, a specific kind of aural place is born, a place that is 'generated by the temporality of the auditory' (Labelle, 2010, p. xvii) – the rural sound idyll.

The rural idyll, although mostly represented in visual ways, inherently also implies an aural environment, which is often constructed in negations to urban sounds: the absence of traffic noise, human and non-human sounds of the busy streets, occasional planes flying by, loud music, construction sounds, etc. In its idealised form, it consists of sounds associated with nature (birdsong, wind, etc.) and other sounds that belong to the sanitised version of countryside discussed above. This ideal environment can be described by the words 'peace', 'quiet', and 'serene', and 'summed up by the concept of tranquillity, which refers to a soothing, calming environment' (Woods, 2011, p. 111). The idea that there is no visual or auditory 'contamination', combined with unspoilt nature is very important to the success of tourism establishments, especially in rural areas, and this is exactly what prospective guests are promised:

> Life in the city is full of stress and noises. That is why we need to escape, to find peace. There is nothing better than to enjoy the beauty of the nature.[6]

Paul Rodaway, too, points out, that for various reasons the natural sound of the 'crashing falls fascinates [people] in a way that the air conditioning motors, for instance, appear not to' (1994, p. 108). The rural sound idyll comprises manifold of sounds: the sounds of animals (birdsong, different insects, domesticated and wild animals), streams and waterfalls, farmyard sounds and weather: wind, rain, thunder, etc. These are what Rodaway (1994, pp. 87–88) calls *soundmarks*, sounds that are recognised and shared by a certain social group. Rodaway also stresses the relatively unique or specific nature of soundmarks to a particular community (i.e. they can encompass the sounds of certain familiar church bells or factory horns). However, I would argue that although this sort of special characteristics might be absent in the sound environments of some particular farms, their respective *individual soundmarks* are what make the sound environment of each studied farm both unique and familiar to the owners of each farm. For example, here are some soundmarks of the aural environment of a tourism farm at around 11 pm in July, as experienced by me:

> The silence consists of birdsong, trees swishing in the wind, insects chirring (crickets? grasshoppers?). ... Jennifer the dog barking now and then. And of course the mosquitoes. The overwhelming twang of mosquitoes that doesn't stop for a moment, stressing the fact that I'm being totally eaten by them and my whole body aches and is covered with red spots. ... A cuckoo is calling, some frogs are croaking. (Kaaristo, sound diary, 2013)

This auditory environment, as characterised by the example above, changes as you move closer to the village, when other sounds join in. When walking from the farm to the village, other sounds emerge, such as cars passing by, the shouts and talk of the people camping at a nearby lake, the rather loud music they are playing and the music from some cars passing by. Reaching the central village of Haanja, there are more cars and more people passing by. The birdsong is still prevalent, except during the weekend, when the sounds of lawnmowers and trimmers can be heard from many directions, making the sounds of different actors all blend into one auditory environment that is not necessarily always characterised by its quietness.

In her article 'The Meaning of Peace and Quiet in Norway', Gullestad (1990, p. 41) discusses the notions of 'peace' and 'quiet' in Norwegian everyday contexts, stating that 'together they constitute a cultural category, intrinsic to social identity and action in the world'. This rings true for Estonians as well, or at least for the tourism farmers I have spoken with, as at one point in my fieldwork I noticed the topic (or trope) of *rahu ja vaikus* ('peace and quiet') being repeated many times during our discussions. Just as Gullestad distinguishes several areas of peace and quiet where these notions are applied – describing personal qualities or people, emotional states, social actions and relations, and objects – similar ideas play an important role in the Estonian tourism farmers' everyday life. A farmer (M, 38) explained that he likes to live in his village 'because of this sense of peace', which is mainly connected to him placing a lot of value on privacy. Another research participant (M, 50) stated very clearly that he has a type of 'ideal guest', as he put it, and that is someone who 'loves nature, quiet and peace'. Analogous ideas were vocalised by many interviewed farmers and, especially after the economic recession, often concern was expressed about how, due to the changed economy and the continuous decrease in the number of guests, they could not 'hand-pick' the guests any more, as they had been able to do only a couple of years earlier.

The perceived 'peace' of the rural environment is something that I discovered and I had noted down in my fieldwork diary too, well before my research focus turned to aural environments. As it turns out, I too must have been somewhat an 'ideal guest' for my hosts, as I seem to have had exactly the experience that was expected of me, so carefully laid out by the hosts:

> You're sitting on the doorstep in front of the house, there's peace and quiet around you (the trees rustle in the wind, and somewhere a bird or two tweets), and you have a cup of coffee with you. ... There is happiness in those moments where you want to be exactly where you are, because you just know: this is perfect and everything is exactly as it's supposed to be. (Kaaristo, field notes 2010)

The feeling described above in my field diary, the sense of perfect belongingness, has very strong auditory aspects. Kaplan (1984, p. 192) suggests the importance of *fascination* when perceiving the natural environment, and how in some natural settings the elements that hold fascination create the sense of tranquillity via being 'calming and quieting: the rustle of leaves, a sunlit raindrop, the view of the woods or of a flowering meadow'. This is complemented by a second major factor that provides restorative experience, *coherence*, which according to Kaplan and Talbot (1983, as cited in Kaplan, 1984, p. 192) is 'the result of organization, of finding a way to put pieces together into a meaningful whole'. While the fascination seems more of a multisensory experience with strong auditory aspects to it, the sense of coherence is more visual, relying heavily on what meets the eye: the trimmed lawn at a (tourism) farm, wheat fields, forests, etc. According to Kaplan, fascination and coherence have to occur together in order to achieve a true restorative experience, a sense of 'being in a whole other world' and the rural sound idyll is one possible environment for such experiences.

Competing values: power over sound

To achieve the desired auditory environment, the rural sound idyll, the surrounding space and the ways it is perceived have to be somewhat arranged by the tourism farmer; some aspects or elements of it need to be downplayed and others reinforced. Tim Edensor argues that, in some tourism situations, activities are supervised in ways that are considered appropriate by the hosts and where 'undesirable elements' and practices, for example loud music playing, 'are likely to be deterred by guards, guides and managers' (Edensor, 2000, p. 328). But this does not necessarily ensure that the guests experience it exactly as intended by the host (Leite & Graburn, 2012, pp. 46–47), which also brings forth the issue of who has the power to control the (aural) environment.

To avoid clashes between hosts' and guests' expectations, hosts use various strategies, such as selecting guests who will appreciate what is offered on their farms. In one of the visited farms, for example, the use of pyrotechnics by the guests is strongly discouraged by the owner of the farm and instead, big bonfires are lit during the night so that the guests can still enjoy a visual spectacle. This is without the loud sounds of fireworks that were disturbing the neighbours, thus 'educating' the guests to appreciate a different kind of aural environment. The owner of that farm (M, 50) commented on this by saying that 'for city people, the silence and the birdsong kill them', and he went on to explain how some guests deal with this discomfort by listening to very loud music or shooting fireworks. According to him, the guests often had to be coaxed into communicating with their surroundings in the 'right' way from his point of view, a position which comprises different elements such as his personal values but also the fact that he has to take into consideration the complaints of his neighbours (both people living nearby but also other tourism farmers who want to secure the 'appropriate' aural environment for their respective guests).

This brings us to the issues of power with regard to the aural environment. In order to ensure their guests the necessary rural sound idyll, hosts also might, for example, avoid doing certain farm chores (especially those involving machinery) before noon because the tourists might be sleeping and the farmers do not want to fill their environment with sounds that are not 'suitable' for this environment, recognising that the rural sound idyll is not only threatened by distinctively urban noises but also by modern everyday rural farming activities, such as tractors ploughing or chainsaws cutting firewood. Tension can arise between the two necessities for the farmers as well; some farmers have shown signs of mild amusement or even irritation with guests who sleep until noon because they are on holiday, a daily routine that presents a contrast to that of the host for whom this is a regular workday. This tension is especially evident on tourism farms where agricultural production is an important source of income for the farm owners, necessitating a reconciliation of their dual roles as farmer and host.

Guests also 'domesticate' the encountered new sound environment, so that it corresponds to their needs and notions of what it is to have a good time. The most common feature of this domestication comes via playing loud music and hence dominating space with sound through the use of (often excessive, from the viewpoint of the host and/or other village dwellers) amplification of a single source of sound. This submerges the pre-existing environment under the blanket of this new dominant sound (Rodaway, 1994, p. 108).

This is especially the case with guests whom the tourism farmers call 'partiers' (*pidut-sejad*): people who rent farmhouses for the sole purpose of 'partying', which usually involves taking a sauna and consuming alcoholic drinks. These partiers have different motivations, according to the interviewed farmers, and are seldom interested in the recreational activities offered to them by farm owners (hiking, walking, etc.) and definitely do not fit into their category of the 'ideal guest', who loves peace and quiet. The parties of students graduating from high school were especially mentioned in this regard, and many farmers expressed their reluctance to accommodate such events for fear of excessive alcohol consumption by the young people and potential problems caused by it; the neighbours and they themselves being disturbed by the noise, significant property damage during such parties and occasionally the need to involve the police. Some farmers said that when it was time for graduation parties (usually June) and young people called to book the houses, they regularly said they were booked. However, for economic reasons, not all tourism farmers can do this, and they accommodate the parties whose look on the appropriate sound environment differs significantly from their own.

In cases like this, different frameworks of cultural and social preferences and values come into play. For the interviewed farmers, their aural environment is something to be enjoyed and also respected – a perspective that clashes with some of their guests who do not share the same values. The reasons for this can vary; for example, Tacchi (2012 [1998]) has demonstrated how the perceived silence can be both positive and negative, depending on the context and timing. In certain circumstances, silence can be undesired; for some people an aural environment without distinctive familiar sounds, for example radio or a TV, can signify isolation, loneliness or boredom. Various sound acts can create an environment of homeliness and the sound from, for example, radio 'can be seen to fill "empty" space and "empty" time with a familiar routine' (Tacchi (2012 [1998]). Thus, by adding their own sounds (i.e. music or the radio) to the rural aural environment, the guests might just be attempting to make their environments more familiar, home-like. But the very same sound act can be seen as 'music' or 'noise' by different people. The individual sound zones (of hosts and guests) that emerge in the particular sound environment can thus be not only overlapping, but also conflicting. The aural environments, comprising various sound acts, some 'natural' and others artificial (or perceived as such), some downplayed, others enhanced, sometimes have to be negotiated between the host and the guest. A farm owner (M, 50) noted, in a somewhat ironic manner, that the guests 'just have to' listen to radio or music albums that they have brought with them, 'something that would make as much noise as possible so that they wouldn't hear the [natural] sounds that surround them'. Another farm owner (F, 50 s) is more relaxed; the music, however loud, does not exactly bother her (though she mostly maintains control over it); her notion of 'peace and quiet' is having no TVs in the house.

According to other tourism farmers the search for a different environment, for 'peace and quiet', can sometimes involve negative elements, in that the encountered environment is something strange and so out of the ordinary that people do not necessarily have the tools to deal with it. The guests may encounter a wide variety of incentives which can evoke a range of emotions, so that 'often, tourists feel that such sites exert power over them and destabilize their identity' (Picard, 2012). One of the tourism farm owners described what, according to her claim, happened to many of her guests on quite a regular basis, in the following way:

> Our guests can go hiking near the Piusa [River]; my husband takes them. There's no special trail there and the nature is truly terrific. You really feel that you're alone. Actually, people are so estranged from themselves; they get scared, and they're afraid of themselves. They get nervous, and feel that something is not right. And then we have to calm them down, with tea for example. And when they get nervous they need to switch on some noise. Because they don't understand what's happening to them. They wake up in the middle of the night quite often and don't understand what's going on. This happens in the winter, not the summer. And then they understand – it's the complete silence. Because we have complete

silence here in the wintertime. It's the same as in the forest: you meet yourself. It scares them. (F, 55)

This compares well to the 'tourist moment', an epiphanic experience, 'spontaneous instance of self-discovery as well as a feeling of communal belonging elicited by serendipity' (Cary, 2004, p. 64). Via such narratives the tourism farmers create a specific kind of rurality, the rural idyll, with its different aural quality they perceive on their farms. The farmers dwell in their soundscapes, perceiving them through different modes of practice that add a different quality to their life-worlds. Therefore, the personal experience of the host is one of the most important aspects when creating and mediating experiences for visitors. By doing this, they construct both ideal rurality – the rural sound idyll – and a notion of the ideal guest. Thus some guests and some ruralities are excluded and others included. The authors of these aural environments are not solely hosts or guests; it is not necessarily the tourist triggering local responses but the host in conversation with their guests 'recreating' the rural sound idyll.

Conclusion

The tourism farmers lean on their values when they make choices and decisions regarding their auditory environments and these choices make their actions and decisions meaningful. The interviewed tourism farmers value the sense of silence, the 'peace and quiet' – the atmospheric value that can be converted into a commercial one – the perceived peaceful countryside that is offered to potential guests. This does not mean that the outside demand for rural tranquillity is the sole reason for the farmers to modify their aural environments. The farm owners' own personal values and ideas about rurality and what it means to live in the countryside play a role here too and both the hosts' and guests' systems of meaning are interconnected when the rural sound idyll is created. The sound idyll is of course also a disputed ground, for there are many different stakeholders there with their own interests in mind and the guests' ideas of the suitable aural environment does not always match with the one of the hosts'. When arranging and (re)creating this environment, some elements are brought into the foreground while others are downplayed and when the values of hosts, guests and other locals living nearby clash, different regimes of value emerge.

Contemporary rural entrepreneurs interpret their environments, constructing both the notions and ideas of rurality and the ideal tourist. The notion of 'peace and quiet', which tourism farmers regard as an important quality of their aural surroundings, is of key importance here. This idea plays a major role when the rural sound idyll is created. The value produced through the intangible and atmospheric natural resources is the result of the interchange of various constructions of rurality by the tourism farmers, who create and recreate their respective sound idylls and mediate them to their guests. These constructions of rurality, which have been developing through the interaction of each individual's values, influence the lived experiences of the tourism farmers and thus, by extension, their guests and their general (rural) environment. The cultural, social and economic values that are embodied in the intangible 'commodities' are traded between the hosts and guests and, as a result, the auditory environment is changed in the process.

Acknowledgements

I am very grateful to all the participants of TOCOCU conference 'Regimes of Value in Tourism' in Sion, Switzerland, 2012 for their feedback on the first version of this paper presented there and to

Dr Aet Annist, Dr Émilie Crossley, and Prof. Art Leete for their comments and suggestions on various drafts of this article.

Manuscript sources

Interviews (recordings and transcripts) and field diaries from Võru County, Estonia (the Haanja, Rõuge, Võru and Vastseliina municipalities), 2008, 2010 and 2013 (in the possession of the author).

Funding

This research was supported by the European Union through the European Regional Development Fund [Centre of Excellence, CECT].

Notes

1. This is illustrated on a homepage of one of the visited tourism farms, where old farmhouses from the end of the 19th century and the beginning of the twentieth century are very visibly arranged and refurnished in such way as to meet the needs and standards of the contemporary tourist, together with the slogan: 'If old Estonians had had motels, the best of them would have been like this'. Retrieved January 20, 2014, from http://www.haanjamehetalu.ee/est/tut
2. Arcadia is a Greek province in Peloponnese region. Already in early history, it was depicted in poetry as idyllic rural land. The start of the Arcadian tradition in the West starts with the Renaissance when court nobility, clergy and other members of the elite started to idealise rural life. The tradition of appreciating nature, which reflects in the landscape painting and ideas of rural idyll in literature, reached new heights in Romanticism (van Koppen, 2000, p. 304).
3. According to the Estonian Tourism Law (§23(3)), in the name of a guest house, hostel, camp or bread and breakfast located in a rural area, the word 'tourism farm' (*turismitalu*) can be used.
4. I will use Võro as the English equivalent for the endonym *võrokõnõ*. On Võro linguistic identities, see Brown (2008).
5. Setomaa (Setoland), with its distinctive culture, and heavily promoted in Estonian tourism, covers a part of the studied Võru County, but I have interviewed only the tourism farmers who identify themselves as Võros. On some aspects of Seto identity, see Leete (2010), and for a discussion of the commodification of Seto culture in tourism, see Annist (2013). There is some tension sometimes between the two neighbouring regions when competing for tourists in conditions of economic recession. Those Setos, they have the [folk] clothes and the religion so they're visually very distinguishable', a research participant once told me with half-joking and half-serious bitterness. 'We the Võros don't have anything like that; we only have the language [Võro dialect], so we have to try extra hard [to succeed in tourism].
6. From the English version of the homepage of a farm, wording unchanged. Retrieved August 8, 2013, from http://www.kobakutalu.com/index2.html

References

Abram, S. (2003). The rural gaze. In P. Cloke (Ed.), *Country visions* (pp. 31–50). Harlow: Pearson Education Limited.
Annist, A. (2013). Heterotopia and Hegemony: Power and culture in Setomaa. *Journal of Baltic Studies*, 44(2), 249–269. doi:10.1080/01629778.2013.775853
Appadurai, A. (1986). Introduction: Commodities and the politics of value. In A. Appadurai (Ed.), *The social life of things: Commodities in cultural perspective* (pp. 3–63). Cambridge: Cambridge University Press.
Ardel, T. (2004). *Maaturismi aabits*. Tallinn: Argo.
Bilsky, W., & Schwartz, S. H. (1994). Values and personality. *European Journal of Personality, 8*, 163–181. doi:10.1002/per.2410080303
Brown, K. (2008). Regional identity and schools in Estonia: Creating a 'We' feeling? *European Education, 40*(3), 8–26. doi:10.2753/EUE1056-4934400301
Bull, M., & Back, L. (Eds.). (2003). *The auditory culture reader*. Oxford: Berg.

Busby, G., & Rendle, S. (2000). The transition from tourism on farms to farm tourism. *Tourism Management, 21*(6), 635–642. doi: 10.1016/S0261-5177(00)00011-X

Crouch, D. (1999). Introduction: Encounters in leisure/tourism. In D. Crouch (Ed.), *Leisure/tourism geographies: Practices and geographical knowledge* (pp. 1–16). London: Routledge.

Dann, G. (1994). Tourism and nostalgia: Looking forward to going back. *Vrijetijd En Samenleving, 12* (1/2), 75–94.

Dicks, B. (2003). *Culture on display. The production of contemporary visitability.* Maidenhead: Open University Press.

Edensor, T. (2000). Staging tourism. Tourists as performers. *Annals of Tourism Research, 27*(2), 322–344. doi:10.1016/S0160-7383(99)00082-1

Edensor, T. (2006). Sensing tourist spaces. In C. Minca & T. Oakes (Eds.), *Travels in paradox: Remapping tourism* (pp. 23–45). Lanham: Rowman & Littlefield.

Farrell, H., & Russell, S. (2011). Rural tourism. In P. Robinson, S. Heitmann, & P. Dieke (Eds.), *Research themes for tourism* (pp. 100–113). Wallingford & Cambridge, MA: CABI.

Grubbström, A., & Soovāli-Sepping, H. (2012). Estonian family farms in transition: A study of intangible assets and gender issues in generational succession. *Journal of Historical Geography, 38,* 329–339. doi:10.1016/j.jhg.2012.03.001

Gullestad, M. (1990). Doing interpretive analysis in a modern large scale society: The meaning of peace and quiet in Norway. *Social Analysis: The International Journal of Social and Cultural Practice, 29,* 38–61.

Henning, D. H. (1974). *Environmental policy and administration.* New York: American Elsevier.

Hoggart, K. (1990). Let's do away with rural. *Journal of Rural Studies, 6*(3), 245–257. doi:10.1016/ 0743-0167(90)90079-N

Hom Cary, S. (2004). The tourist moment. *Annals of Tourism Research, 31*(1), 61–77.

Jamal, T., & Robinson, M. (2012). Introduction: The evolution and conteporary positioning of tourism as a focus of study. In T. Jamal & M. Robinson (Eds.), *The SAGE handbook of tourism studies* (pp. 1–16). Los Angeles: Sage.

Kaaristo, M., & Järv, R. (2012). 'Our clock moves at a different pace': The Timescapes of identity in Estonian rural tourism. – *Folklore. Electronic Journal of Folklore, 51,* 109–132. doi:10.7592/ FEJF2012.51.kaaristo-jarv

Kahn, D. (1999). *Noise, water, meat: A history of sound in the arts.* Cambridge, MA: MIT Press.

Kaplan, R. (1984). Impact of urban nature: A theoretical analysis. *Urban Ecology, 8,* 189–197.

Kaplan, S., & Talbot, J. F. (1983). Psychological benefits of a wilderness experience. In I. Altman & J. F. Wohlwill (Eds.), Behavior and the Natural Environment (pp. 163–204). New York, NY: Plenum.

van Koppen, K. (2000). Resource, Arcadia, Lifeworld. Nature concepts in environmental sociology. *Sociologia Ruralis, 40*(3), 300–318.

Labelle, B. (2010). *Acoustic territories. Sound culture and everyday life.* London: Continuum.

Lane, B. (2012). Rural tourism: An overview. In T. Jamal & M. Robinson (Eds.), *Handbook of tourism studies* (pp. 354–370). London: Sage.

Leete, A. (2010). Geopolitics and ethnology. The Setu Case. In J. Lehtonen & S. Tenkanen (Eds.), *Ethnology in the 21st century. Transnational reflections of past, present and future* (pp. 35–47). Turku: University of Turku.

Leite, N., & Graburn, N. (2012). Anthropological interventions in tourism studies. – *The SAGE handbook of tourism studies.* In T. Jamal & M. Robinson (Eds.), *Handbook of tourism studies* (pp. 35–64). London: Sage.

Nugin, R. (2014). 'I think that they should go. Let them see something'. The context of rural youth's out-migration in post-socialist Estonia. *Journal of Rural Studies, 34,* 51–64. doi:http://dx.doi.org/ 10.1016/j.jrurstud.2014.01.003

Picard, D. (2012). Tourism, Awe and Inner Journeys. In D. Picard & M. Robinson (Eds.), *Emotion in motion. Tourism, affect and transformation* (pp. 1–19). Farnham: Ashgate.

Rodaway, P. (1994). *Sensuous geographies. Body, sense and place.* London: Routledge.

Tacchi, J. (2012 [1998]). Radio texture: Between self and others. In D. Miller (Ed.), *Material cultures: Why some things matter* (pp. 25–45). London: UCL Press.

Tuohino, A., & Pitkänen, K. (2004). The transformation of a Neutral Lake landscape into a meaningful experience – interpreting tourist photos. *Journal of Tourism and Cultural Change, 2*(2), 77–93. doi:10.1080/14766820408668170

Urry, J. (2002 [1990]). *The tourist gaze.* Lancaster: Sage.

Veijola, S., & Jokinen, E. (1994). The body in tourism. *Theory, Culture & Society, 11*(3), 125–151. doi:10.1177/026327694011003006

Võsu, E., & Kaaristo, M. (2009). An ecological approach to contemporary rural identities: The case of tourism farms in South-East Estonia. *Journal of Ethnology and Folkloristics, 3*(1), 73–94.

Weeden, C. (2011). Responsible tourist motivation: How valuable is the Schwartz value survey? *Journal of Ecotourism, 10*(3), 214–234. doi:10.1080/14724049.2011.617448

Woods, M. (2011). *Rural*. London: Routledge.

From tourist to person: the value of intimacy in touristic Cuba

Valerio Simoni

Centre for Research in Anthropology (CRIA), Lisbon University Institute, Lisbon, Portugal

Building on tourism scholarship on existential authenticity, touristic intimacy, and the limitations of the tourist role, the article provides an empirically grounded analysis of how the value of intimacy was expressed and negotiated in the course of encounters between foreign tourists and members of the visited population in Cuba. Tourism-related identifications in this Caribbean country are shaped by local notions of tourism hustling and pose a challenge to the development of mutually gratifying relationships between tourists and Cubans. The exploration of Cubans' concerns and informal ways of approaching tourists, and of the ways in which friendships, partying, and sexual engagements between them were enacted, highlights the efforts of the protagonists of these encounters to achieve relationships that could help them move beyond negative identifications and lead to the recognition of their individuality and shared humanity as persons. Intimacy appears as a fundamental regime of value informing these processes. The reflections that the article develops on the concrete manifestations of intimacy in touristic encounters and the kind of alliances it prompted open the way for further research on the role played by international tourism in the diffusion and actualization of this regime of value.

Introduction

'For me you are not a tourist. You are a person, a human being!'[1] In the course of my field-work in Cuba, I repeatedly heard this statement from Cubans who were interacting with foreign tourists. Such a claim raises a series of questions that I would like to use as a point of departure for this article. What did such contrast between a tourist and a person entail? Why would anyone refer to it? And what were its effects on tourist–Cuban encounters? My aim here is to provide some answers to these questions and address their implications for our understanding of tourism and the forms of subjectivity and regimes of value that can emerge from it. To do so, the article considers how the value of intimacy was expressed and intersubjectively negotiated in the course of encounters between foreign tourists and members of the visited population in Cuba.[2] My argumentation will proceed inductively and be grounded in the discussion of a range of empirical examples that bring us from the initial moments of such encounters to the establishment of friend-ships, festive, and sexual relationships.

To contrast a tourist with a person may seem rather striking to the reader. After all, are not all tourists also persons? As other scholars of tourism have shown, it is rather common for the term 'tourist' to be 'imbued in contemporary understandings with a culturally derogative and negative connotation' (McCabe, 2005, p. 85) and to be 'used as a derisive label' (Brown, 1996, p. 38). At least since MacCannell's groundbreaking publication of *The Tourist* (1976), there has been much recognition of the ambivalence and paradoxes inherent in the possibility of being someone – a tourist – that seeks authenticity in travel but is simultaneously aware that 'authenticity is only achievable outside the realm of the tourist role' (Olsen, 2002, p. 160). Hom Cary's reflection on the 'tourist moment' addresses a similar tension in the 'interpellation' and 'collective subjectivity of the tourist' (2004, p. 62). Her focus is on the serendipity of 'tourist moments' in which the tourists' search for authenticity is temporarily fulfilled (2004, p. 66). The tourist moment is an instance of simultaneous interpellation and dissolution of 'the tourist as subject' (p. 69); 'a liminal moment in which the "tourist has ceased to be a tourist" (Ryan, 1991, p. 35)' (p. 64). In touristic encounters in Cuba, the enactment of intimacy enabled a similar dissolution of the tourist role, bringing to the fore other forms of subjectivity.

In theorizing the tourist moment, Hom Cary builds on Wang's conceptualization of 'existential authenticity' (1999), 'a special state of Being in which one is true to oneself, and acts as a counterdose to the loss of "true self" in public roles and public spheres in modern Western society (Berger, 1973)' (p. 358). Proposing an alternative take to this notion, Olsen (2002) encourages us 'to pay attention to the actual contexts where' the creation of 'a feeling of authenticity in individuals' is at work (p. 160). This author points to the need of moving beyond 'essentialist and existentialist perspectives that merely observe that such experiences are found' (Olsen, 2002, p. 160) and result from the generalized alienation of the modern subject, advocating instead the adoption of a constructivist approach (Bruner, 1994; Cohen, 1988) that analyses 'these processes in their making' (p. 165), in an empirically grounded manner. We rejoin here McCabe's call to investigate 'what people achieve by deploying concepts like "tourist" in their constructions of themselves and the activities of others' (2005, p. 85). According to Olsen (2002), 'the tourist role is one of several accessible roles' in tourism, one 'that individuals enter in distinct contexts and not an all-embracing feature imposed from a structural level' (p. 169). He then goes on to consider experiences in tourism where the tourist role has been altered, dismissed, and altogether overcome. The value of such experiences, their 'authenticity' in Olsen's case, is intimately tied to this ability to go beyond such a role to enact other ones. Along similar lines, Sant Cassia reflects on tourists in Malta striving to 'personalize their interaction' with hosts and 'transform their role' so as to become 'more individuals and less "mere tourists"' (1999, p. 253); an assessment that leads him to consider that '[t]ourism aims at the individuation of the self through the authentication of experience' (p. 253).

While in this article I am not directly focusing on the issue of authenticity and its existential version, I find it useful to situate my argumentation in continuity with this scholarship, and in particular with the reflections on the perceived limitations of the tourist role and the ensuing drive to reach beyond it in order to access something of value. Moving from philosophical reasoning to a more empirically grounded analysis, the article starts by showing the contingent emergence of the tourist role in a specific realm of tourism interactions in Cuba, considering how this role was shaped by local semantic fields and ways of framing, most notably Cuban notions of tourism hustling. Having recognized this relational characterization of the tourist, the core of the article focuses on how the enactment of intimacy in the course of interactions between foreign visitors and members of the Cuban population enabled its demise and the emergence of more valuable forms of subjectivity. Intimacy, in this sense, appears as a key regime of value informing these interactions and the subject formations that resulted from them.[3]

In her insightful book *Being a Tourist*, Harrison (2003) develops the notion of 'touristic intimacy' and shows the importance that the value of intimacy can acquire as a driver of people's travel. Drawing on her conceptualization, Frohlick (2007) argues that '[t]ouristic intimacy is ... part of a larger quest for connection that tourists seek in crossing international borders and is also the moral discourse that serves to justify international travel as a means through which cross-cultural understandings are gained' (p. 152). Harrison goes as far as suggesting that we reconsider MacCannell's view of the tourist as seeking the authentic in the places visited by shifting the emphasis from places to 'the sociability, perchance the intimacy, that one encounters while travelling' (2003, p. 90). While much of her focus is on the connections tourists make with other fellow travellers, Harrison also reflects on tourists' expectations of 'meeting the local people' (2003, pp. 61–66), their desire to engage, however briefly and incidentally, with residents of the visited destination. The value of such 'human connection' (see also Picard, 2011) was cherished by Harrison's research participants, as was the fact that, '[i]f only momentarily, each was separated out from the generic category of "stranger", and seen as a real person' (2003, p. 65). It is such desire 'to connect with others ... to reaffirm a fuller sense of their individual humanity' (2003, p. 47, see the parallel with Sant Cassia's remarks on individuation above) that I would like to retain here, given that it resonates strongly with my ethnographic material from Cuba. Whereas Harrison and her tourist interlocutors are left wondering about how the 'locals' viewed these same relations, my work in Cuba indicates that the claim of sharing a common humanity, and the related desire for individuation, were also strong among members of the visited population and an extremely valued dimension of such encounters (see Simoni, 2013).

However, as far as touristic encounters in Cuba were concerned, achieving intimacy and a sense of human connection was not a straightforward task. Other framings and categorizations tended to prevail, obstructing tourists' and Cubans' recognition of each other as individuated persons. Rather than the generic category of 'stranger' referred to by Harrison, the more specific ones of 'tourist' on the one hand and of '*jinetero/a*' (tourist-rider) or 'tourist hustler' on the other often stood in the way of achieving the kind of intimacies to which both tourists and their Cuban interlocutors could aspire.[4] From the Spanish *jinete* (jockey, rider), *jineterismo* evoked in post-soviet Cuba the riding of foreigners for instrumental purposes and was often associated with notions of tourism hustling and prostitution.[5] For Palmié (2004), in much popular discourse *jineterismo* 'speaks to morally highly ambiguous notions about commoditized exchange, luxury consumption, and the creation of social identities through processes of objectification' (p. 243). Following this frame of legibility, the 'victims' of such objectification became the tourists, cast as preys of deceptive *jineteros* and *jineteras* who rode them for purely instrumental motives. As I have argued elsewhere (Simoni, 2014a), by the time I undertook my fieldwork in Cuba, the narrative of *jineterismo* had gone global, and informed tourists' expectations towards the prospect of meeting Cuban people, generating scepticism, doubts, and a climate of suspicion about each other's agendas.

Given this state of affairs, it is easy to imagine that the establishment of the kind of intimacy and human connection referred to by Harrison (2003) was not straightforward for most tourists in Cuba. The simple impression that Cubans were approaching you as yet another mere tourist could immediately bring to life the spectre of *jineterismo*, and with it the worry of being treated as a type and instrumentalized as an object. The context in which I worked in Cuba seems to support the notion of the 'tourist role ... as an asymmetrical counterconcept' to the ideals of 'intimacy and closeness in relations' (Olsen, 2002, p. 168). Therefore there was a need, for tourists and Cubans who cherished such ideals, to bring about other categories of the self (beyond those of tourist and *jinetero/a*) and other ways of engaging with each other – categories and ways that could enable their relationships to move forward without surrendering to paralyzing suspicion and mistrust.

Addressing tourists as persons

In his seminal article on Sri Lankan street guides, Crick remarks that '[t]ourists wary of being cheated in a foreign country may react gratefully to "Hello friend", a common conversational opening by the street guides' (1992, p. 139). In Cuba too, '*hola amigo*' was a common way to address visitors in the streets. However, especially after a few days spent on the island, such immediate expressions of friendliness also contributed to raise doubts about the motives of the diffuse cordiality. Much like in the Turkish context in which Tucker carried out her research, where tourists were often 'suspicious of the perceived over-friendliness of salesmen and waiters' (2001, p. 880), visitors in Cuba too grew tired of Cuban's over-friendly approaches. Accordingly, the question of how best to address visitors called for inventiveness and subtlety. With certain types of 'openings' (*entradas*) becoming more and more common and widespread – 'hello friend' and 'where are you from' the most frequent ones (see Simoni, 2008b) – the impression of serendipity risked to fade away, together with the promise of a genuine and personal encounter with ordinary Cubans. Keeping such promise alive, Cubans deployed other approaches that preserved a sense of something special, of an encounter like no other.

Their ability to decode the tourists' behaviour and detect their potential interests could help such personalization. This is what Fernando, a self-professed *ex-jinetero* in his 30s, explained as he delighted me with a didactic tour of Havana, a tour enlivened by concrete examples of the approaches he would adopt. Passing by a tourist couple who were busy taking pictures on the Malecón, Havana's famous seaside promenade, for instance, Fernando told me how he could have opened an interaction. As if on his way somewhere, he would casually stop by and show some interest for the angle the tourists had chosen for their picture, dropping a remark on the practice of photography and his fondness for this art, and eventually adding a couple of tips and suggestions. This was likely to capture the tourists' attention and enable him to move forward with a conversation. Similarly, tourists who were consulting a guidebook could be suitably approached by asking whether they needed any direction or help, and so on and so forth. More generally, Fernando made it clear through his various examples that understanding one's focus of attention and devising openings dotted with remarks and suggestions that fitted creatively into that focus was a smart and successful way of getting in touch with tourists. Again, what seemed very important was to avoid giving any hint of premeditations, any suggestion of being a full-time *jinetero* intent on deceiving the typical 'tourist dupe'. His openings were precisely designed not to give the impression of the well-scripted and predictable *jinetero*-type of approach. They were to be seen as a genuine expression of interest that treated each tourist as a particular individual, with his own specific personality, interests, and agendas.

For my friend Ernesto, a Cuban man in his 20s with whom I spent much time hanging around in Havana, what mattered most for success in engaging with foreign tourists was 'to be a mind' (*ser una mente*): being smart and intelligent, knowing about people, about relationships, about sentiments – 'working the truth' (*trabajar la verdad*) of these things. As he put it, the 'struggle' (*lucha*) to get tourists in Havana's streets (*en la calle*) – a competitive world full of 'wickedness' (*maldad*) – was a struggle in which the sharpest mind would prevail, in which the experience and knowledge gained *en la calle* became paramount. The source of many of his colleagues' mistakes in dealing with tourists, according to Ernesto, was that they thought of themselves as superior, being vain (*vanos*) and looking down at tourists as if they were *bobos* (stupid, naïve). This was a major error of judgement, he maintained, and one that went on to colour Cubans' ways of relating with visitors, framing them in typifications and objectifications that the latter were deemed to sense and resent. Instead, advocated Ernesto, one had to remain open and respect the fully fledged humanity and individuality of every tourist. Such personalization was also a call, for tourists, to reciprocate by treating him in the same way, not as an alleged *jinetero* and 'hustler', but as a human being with comparable moral and emotional qualities, desires, and aspirations.

Friendship and mutuality among human beings

As mentioned above, appeals to friendship were among the most common openings deployed by Cubans to catch the tourists' attention. Far from being straightforwardly endorsed by visitors, (over-)friendly openings could generate increased scepticism and suspicion, especially when deployed too loosely and without any apparent effort to substantiate them. Particularly among those tourists that spent several weeks travelling around Cuba, many were those who were led to conclude that Cubans met in the streets, particularly in tourism areas, were generally interested in their money – 'when they look at us they see the dollar sign!' – and that this interest was often 'hidden' behind an exaggerated and contrived friendliness. The approach adopted thus seemed to rely on a 'front–back' opposition akin to that theorized by Goffman (1959), and further elaborated in MacCannell's notion of 'staged authenticity' in relation to tourist settings (1973, 1976), the rationale being that behind Cubans' front, behind their superficial 'show' of friendliness, lay the more 'real' back of instrumental agendas.

The visitors' reactions to such immediate professions of friendliness ranged from complete disregard for the Cuban at stake (it could be less embarrassing to pretend not to have heard a friendly call than to openly deny its significance) to more positive responses that granted them at least the benefit of doubt. In the latter case, even sceptical tourists could playfully get along with the relationships while remaining high on guard, keeping under check their engagements so as not to risk too much and incur too big a disappointment. On their side, Cubans could struggle to make sense of tourists' engagements and to evaluate the intensity of their commitment. For them, the visitors' scepticism, their inability to let go, 'open up' (*abrirse*), and trust them, could be rather disappointing, as it hampered the possibility of developing more gratifying and beneficial relationships.

In spite of widespread scepticism, many tourists I met also valued the idea of meeting the locals, of getting to know ordinary people, people with whom they could talk, for instance, about the realities of everyday life in Cuba, and develop relations that could help them move 'backstage', beyond the tautological connotations of the 'tourist bubble'. Capitalizing on these expectations, Cubans could quickly remind tourists that they had come to Cuba to discover their country and its people, and therefore 'had to' meet and make friends with the locals. The right attitude prescribed here was to open up and trust, if one wished to gain access to the real Cuba and move beyond the glossy images of tourism brochures. Typical tourism narratives of cross-cultural communication and understanding were thus activated to build closer connections with tourists. These 'friendliness-/trust-arousing' discourses were constructing tourism, tourists and processes of touristification in their wake, affirming hierarchies between different tourist practices, and touching the sensitive issue of tourists' agency and freedom.

Bringing the visitors' attention to the limitations of the 'typical-tourist' role and its normative dimensions – in terms, for instance, of being channelled into the routes and circuits provided and suggested by the industry – these narratives tended to strike a right note, triggering sympathetic and consensual reactions. A common follow up to these encouragements to trust and make friends with ordinary Cubans were suggestions that opened up new fields of possibility, foreshowing for instance unforgettable and unique experiences off the beaten track. This was also when Cubans could try and take the lead in their relationship with visitors, at least in terms of decision-making. Enacting the quintessential 'local' and banking on their insider knowledge, they would encourage their foreign companions to follow them not as tourists but as friends, to listen to their intimate stories of everyday Cuba and make the most of experiences out of the tourists' reach.

Several foreigners I spoke to were seduced by such narratives and positively surprised by the immediate friendliness and helpfulness of their Cuban friends. Was this a Cuban typicality? As two French women told me, on their first approach Cubans seemed indeed to be extremely kind and welcoming, and it was impressive how one could get very quickly very deep in incredibly intense and intimate relationships (*'ça va très vite très profond!'*). Advising tourists on where to shop, eat and drink if they wished to save money, sharing confidences about the hardship of everyday life on the island, inviting visitors to have food in their homes or some 'hidden' restaurant that was not in any official tourist map – by doing all that Cubans gained the amity, complicity and trust of their foreign partners and were able to bring about other types of identifications that went beyond the typical 'tourist'-'*jinetero/a*' dyad.

Generosity could easily be cast as an important indication of a genuine friendship. Among the people whom I noticed were particularly keen to invite and share with tourists what they had, were the members of the Rasta[6] clique that hung around Havana's tourism areas. They were used to the company of young travellers and backpackers, which tended to have open-ended travel plans and looked forward to the possibility of engaging with locals and getting closer to their everyday lives. Converging with these tourists' aspirations was the Rasta's professed aversion for 'touristy places' and their praise of a simple lifestyle. Common were the critiques of the commercialism of tourism installations, as epitomized by those establishments that made business out of 'prostitution' and the selling of expensive and price-inflated *mojitos*, the cocktail on which *jineteros/as* were allegedly gaining the highest commissions. As an alternative to this, the Rasta could suggest to gather collectively some money and purchase a bottle of rum for everyone to share, including the foreign friends. Something to 'share, the Cuban way' (compartir, a lo cubano) sitting on the wall of the Malecón. When accompanying tourists, the emphasis would then be on going 'to the places of the Cubans', so that visitors could save money, avoiding expensive 'tourist-only' locations. 'No one is a tourist with us; we are all the same, human beings', was among the sentences supporting these endeavours. Such moments of friendship could be contrasted with the behaviour of other ill-intentioned Cubans, who treated tourists as dupes (i.e. as tourists) and brought them to expensive tourist bars and restaurants in return for commissions. Partaking in these moments of sociability with their Rasta companions, the visitors could easily give in the professed friendship.

This valorization of an intimacy that strived to go beyond the tourist and *jinetero/a* typifications resonated strongly with Julien, a Canadian teenager with whom I spent a few days towards the end of his one month stay in Cuba. Julien had mismanaged his holiday budget and after a couple of weeks of excessive spending had had to rely, to get by, on the understanding and generosity of those Cuban people and friends who were able to recognize his predicament – his 'being like them', 'having nothing', as he put it when reflecting on his lack of economic resources. Among the many Cubans he had known, it was those who had been generous to him (occasionally offering a drink, some food) and had not treated him as a privileged tourist, which had become his friends. Such acts of generosity had 'warmed his heart' (*chauffé le cœur*) and made him want to give back and reciprocate. After several disappointing encounters with 'cheaters' earlier in his journey, people who had treated him as a mere tourist, Julien had managed to discover 'more authentic relationships' and what he called 'intimacy': the state of 'feeling good with somebody' (*être bien avec une personne*).

In the sentence with which I opened this article – 'For me you are not a tourist. You are a person, a human being!' – the accent was once again on grounding relationships in the fundamental commonality of the people involved. Rather than being catalogued, discriminated, and targeted in dichotomous ways on the base of their assumed (privileged) status and the asymmetry of resources – so the reasoning went – tourists deserved to be recognized, understood, and treated for what they were as persons, with all their peculiarities, idiosyncrasies, and unique circumstances and ways of being (we can hear echoes here of Ernesto's warning not to treat tourists as stupid rich *bobos*). This, of course, was also a call for tourists to reciprocate and do the same with their Cuban friends, as opposed to confining them to a world of *jineterismo* and *jinetero/a* identifications. The moral demand at stake here was for tourists to step out of a world governed by structural inequalities, of interpretations of each other's behaviour in terms of inescapable instrumentality, and to commit oneself to a fully fledged friendship; one that would respect the integrity of the other, its sheer complexity, and not reduce him or her to a type, a summative account, a partial representation and example of a more general pattern (see Throop, 2014). We can read this as a call for openness, for partaking in a world yet unwritten and unscripted, full of generative potential in terms of ways of being and doing things together.

As I have elaborated elsewhere (Simoni, 2014c), by insisting on their commitment, or at least their human potential and aspiration to engage in a disinterested, sentiment-based friendship, Cubans engaging informally with foreign visitors were striving to align their moral selves to those of their tourist friends and thus lay claim to the possibility of being together in a shared social world. But this common world was not only a sought after ideal at a moral level; it was a more concrete aspiration too, and one that such friendships could also help bring a little closer. For one, in their attempts to cement intimate bonds with visitors, Cubans were also entangling them into the moral imperatives that came with fully fledged friendship. Itself an 'ethical demand' (Zigon, 2013), friendship, much like love, called for a certain commitment and continuity in the relationship. The responsibilities tourists felt towards their Cuban friends could ultimately help the latter realize other socio-economic aspirations too: never again having to worry about being left in need with no one to turn to, or even being able to travel abroad thanks to a foreign friend. Tourists could help Cubans in this and thus lead to a more tangible narrowing of inequalities too. All in all, such formulations of friendship strived to escape the reductive tourist-*jinetero/-a* dyad and its relational dead ends, to open up new realms of possibilities and unlock other horizons of becoming, imagining common trajectories for the future.

Festive communitas and serendipitous seduction

An examination of the sociabilities that took shape in festive moments sheds light on the potential of these types of engagements to move beyond typified roles and towards more egalitarian subject formations. We enter here a realm of interaction that fits more closely those scholarly readings of tourism that emphasize its potential to engender states of 'liminality', 'communitas', and 'existential authenticity' (see Daniel, 1996; Graburn, 1983, 1989; Hom Cary, 2004; Kim & Jamal, 2007; Wang, 1999). For my Cuban research participants, invitations to take part in parties and festivals were a common way to get in touch and initiate interactions with tourists. For Fernando, '*irse de fiesta*' (go party) signalled a key turn in his interactions with foreigners and was a top priority. Once partying was on the way 'that's it!' he told me, implying that relationships were likely to get increasingly smooth and gratifying: tourists would leave worries behind and become more affable and easy to deal with. A range of opportunities could open up, enabling people like Fernando to have fun and develop rewarding relationships. When Cubans noticed the tourists' reluctance to 'go with the flow', prescriptive suggestions could easily emerge, encouraging visitors to enjoy and indulge in pleasure. The assumption here was that tourists were in Cuba to enjoy themselves: '*hay que disfrutar!*' (one should enjoy!), was the widespread encouragement. It was the trope of 'tourism as the pursuit of pleasure' that was called forth. '*La vida es un carnaval!*' (Life is a carnival!) as the refrain of a song that was often played for tourists put it.

It was common for Cubans who took it as their task to get tourists into a party mood to suggest a venue where people would be able to enjoy and indulge. Once there, they would willingly take on the role of hosts (or second-order hosts) mediating between tourists and bar tenders, waiters, cashiers, and other gatekeepers of goods and services. Their mediation could help keep the tourists 'high' (Graburn, 1989, 2001) and minimize potential disruptions to their good time and euphoria, such as having to consult a map to know where to go, finding out how to get a drink, queuing to place orders, checking menus, prices and bills, and so on – a whole range of situations that could remind tourists of their being a tourist, of their difference, their potential ignorance of local customs, and the ensuing possibility of being cheated. Once festive happenings were in full swing and tourists-sponsored drinks and food flowed, this could also attract people from the immediate surroundings, particularly in open-air settings, who could take their chance and try to join in. The newly arrived would cheerfully stretch out glasses to be filled, toast with those already involved, hugging and shaking hands and blending into the intimate atmosphere of fun, hedonism, and playfulness. But this is when tensions could also arise and boundaries materialize, leading doubtful participants – most notably the paying tourists – to wonder about the relational idiom at stake: who is in this party? Who belongs to the group? Is this a genuine festive happening or are there other motives involved? Is someone profiting from the generous sponsoring of the tourist? Such questions could emerge and crack the party atmosphere, raising doubts about people's intentionality and the values guiding their engagements, about the status of participants and their degree of intimacy, threatening to bring the partners involved back to irreconcilable differences as tourists and Cubans.

The suspicion that someone could just pretend to be cheerful while actually having other agendas in mind could be particularly destabilizing for tourists. A daunting scenario was that Cubans could be working to intoxicate visitors with drinks or other drugs to profit from them – gaining commissions on the things purchased, inviting other Cuban friends at the tourists' expenses, and ultimately trying to get hold of their money and valuables. The emergence of these preoccupations could lead tourists from euphoria to anxiety, to the fear of losing control in the face of mischievous and calculating hustlers: from the feeling of festive communitas among equals, to one of unequal instrumental relationships and exploitation, there was a sense of a possible radical bifurcation in the regimes of value and modes of engagement at stake.

Partying and dancing in Cuba were also key arenas for seduction (Simoni, 2012). In this respect, my explorations of sexual relationships between tourist men and Cuban women show that a favoured way of avoiding negatively connoted categorizations of 'sex tourism' and 'prostitution' was precisely to draw continuities between festivity and seduction, and sexual engagements. Recounting to me their sexual relations with Cuban women, several tourist men placed enormous value in all that happened before intercourse actually took place, namely the process of establishing a pleasant relationship, of having fun together, getting excited, and creating a sense of intimacy. From that, and under the aegis of the same regime of value, the prospect of a genuine, spontaneous sexual relation could materialize. Many tourist men regretted the commoditization of relationships, and more particularly sexual relationships, in present-day touristic Cuba. Ruggiero for instance, a young Italian I briefly met in a disco, nostalgically recalled how six–seven years earlier he had found Cuban people to be much more innocent and naive, whereas now, excluding some areas outside Havana, they were becoming more and more 'like us', 'money oriented', and in the process of 'capitalistizing' [sic] (*capitalizzare*) themselves. It was a sense of ingenuousness, spontaneity, serendipity, and uncalculated relationships growing out of genuine desire to party, enjoy, and be seduced that people like Ruggero seemed to value. Evoked here was also the notion of tourism, and of being like a tourist, as something antithetical to ideals of genuine intimacy (see Olsen, 2002), an intimacy that found its authenticity in serendipity (Hom Cary, 2004).

Smooth continuities and overlaps between a carefree and happy-go-lucky festivity, seduction processes, and sexual relationships were highlighted in the narratives of many tourists I spoke to. Ruggero's view opposed a positively valued (albeit almost vanished) local culture of fun-loving, sexually permissive, and 'hot' Cubans, to the negative transformations for which tourism was held responsible, more particularly its role in the commoditization of sexual relationships and the booming of prostitution. The solution was to get off the beaten track and seek the still hot Cuba (Simoni, 2014b). We are confronted here with one of the long-standing tropes of tourism, characterized by MacCannell (1976) as the quest for authenticity, which in this case took the shape of a pursuit of 'authentic social relations and sociability' (Selwyn, 1996, p. 8), an authenticity to be found in intimacy (Harrison, 2003, p. 90), and more particularly in intimate relations with the authentic 'hot' Cuban (Simoni, 2013).

Besides these endeavours to move beyond tourism and the tourist role to access much valued forms of intimacy, I have also shown elsewhere (Simoni, 2014b) that on some occasions the tourist position and the privileges that could ensue from it could also be embraced by visitors. Such was the stance of the self-professed 'sex tourist', who revelled in the pleasures that his tourist status granted, 'happy to be just a tourist' (McCabe, 2005, p. 99, see also Brown, 1996; Selwyn, 1996), and who scorned the self-righteousness and hypocrisy of other travellers. Mutual forms of intimacy did not seem to matter much, and intimacy, overall, ceased to be a big source of concern and value. What these last considerations point to is the importance, for researchers of tourism, to assess the extent of convergence and intersubjectivity in terms of the regimes of value that inform the establishment of encounters between tourists and the members of the visited population that engage with them. In Cuba, the existence or not of such a confluence was likely to inform the more or less mutual or exploitative character of touristic encounters.

Conclusion

In the realm of tourism in Cuba, the spectre of *jineterismo* threatened to cast the partners involved in touristic encounters as a 'tourist dupe' on the one hand and as a 'deceptive hustler' on the other. The ethnographic material discussed above shows that rather than surrendering to these typifications and the limited scope for intimacy they granted, both tourists and Cubans strived to achieve other relational forms of subjectification and engagement. Intimacy was an ideal that the protagonists of touristic encounters often shared; a regime of value that informed the way their interactions took shape and developed. Their notions of intimacy often stood in direct opposition to those of 'tourism hustling', 'prostitution', and *jineterismo* and brought to the fore a sense of common humanity, of being individuals that deserved to be recognized in all their particularity, unicity, and idiosyncratic qualities rather than as exemplifications of a type. In their ways of approaching tourists, many among my Cuban research participants recognized the importance of this, and called for tourists to treat them the same way, so as to open up possibilities for mutually gratifying relationships.

What can be identified here is tourism's tension and drive to surpass itself, or what has been considered, for more than half a century now, as a central paradox and dialectic informing the development of modern tourism. This is what Enzensberger (1996 [1958]) phrased as 'the yearning for freedom from society' being 'harnessed by the very society it seeks to escape' (p. 129). The ethnographic material discussed above suggests that within touristic encounters lay the potential to break Enzensberger's 'vicious circle of [tourism's] ... inner logic and its confinement' (1996, p. 132), and that human relationships could not be reduced to any deterministic and ineluctable scenario. In the course of their interactions, the tourists and Cubans I referred to in this article negotiated a common regime of value to inform their engagements. They generated alliances that went beyond any reductive reading of the touristic encounters (see Simoni, 2014a) and that emerged and gained force in opposition to tourism-related typifications. Such alliances took shape in a context of unregulated, informal encounters that were haunted by narratives of deception, cheating, and potential exploitation; a context in which the touristic connotation could easily act as a reverse Midas touch, spoiling and tarnishing everything it touched, and projecting a negative light on relations and the subjects involved in them – no longer persons nor humans, as the opening quote suggested.

The notions of friendship, festivity, and seduction that came about in the tourist–Cuban interactions I considered tended to downplay inequalities, and all strived to infuse a sense of mutuality and reciprocity between the protagonists involved. Intimacy appeared as the key value that all these different types of relationalities held in common, on which both tourists and Cubans seemed to converge. However vague and 'thin', and perhaps also because of it, their ideals of intimacy acted as a sort of 'lingua franca in a cultural borderland' (Mattingly, 2006), a minimal common view that enabled them, at the very least, to overcome the limitations of the 'tourist' and 'hustler' typifications that threatened them. The role played by international tourism, and more particularly by the kind of encounters considered here, in the diffusion, actualization, and negotiation of these ideals of intimacy certainly deserves closer scrutiny.

Such intimacy, as a regime of value on which tourists and Cubans seemed to converge, also carried implications that recent anthropological literature on love may help us elucidate. The ability to engage in 'romantic' 'selfless' 'pure' love has been considered a key marker of modernization, and of being an autonomous and self-determined subject.[7] According to Povinelli (2006), it is precisely in love – and in the notions of intimacy considered in this article, we may add – that one may 'locate the hegemonic home of liberal logics and aspirations' (p. 17). In this view, 'the ability to "love" in an "enlightened" way becomes the basis (the "foundational event") for constituting free and self-governing subjects and, thus, "humanity"' (Povinelli, 2004 cited in Faier, 2007, p. 153). When seen in this light, the links between the ideals of intimacy considered in this article and the related forms of subjectification they afforded seem all the more clear. If the protagonists of touristic encounters wished to overcome tourism-related identifications and to engage with each other on the grounds of their individuality and common humanity, there could be hardly any better path to do so than through a common infatuation with the value of intimacy.

Acknowledgements

I am indebted to my research participants for their generous collaboration during fieldwork and also thank Émilie Crossley for her helpful comments and editorial guidance on an earlier version of this paper.

Funding

The research was supported by the Portuguese Foundation for Science and Technology [grant number SFRH/BPD/66483/2009] and by the Swiss National Science Foundation [grant number PZ00P1_147946].

Notes

1. All the empirical quotes appearing in this article have been translated into English by the author and are based on recollections after the events took place.
2. The 12 months' ethnographic fieldwork (mainly participant observation) on which the research is grounded took place between 2005 and 2013 in Havana, the rural town of Viñales (approximately 200 km west of the capital) and the beach resort of Playas del Este (about half an hour by car from Havana).
3. Other regimes of value, most notably an economic one, also played an important role in touristic encounters in Cuba (see Simoni, 2014a). Notwithstanding the importance of understanding the articulations of these different regimes, and of the competing modes of engagement they informed (see Simoni, 2013), in this article I predominantly focus on the value of intimacy.
4. I have discussed elsewhere (Simoni & McCabe, 2008) how, as a foreigner who frequented tourism locations in Cuba, I was also caught in these framings and categorizations, and how this shaped the nature of my fieldwork and of my relationships with Cuban research participants. The anthropologists' long-standing reluctance to be identified with tourists (see Crick, 1995) is another theme that would deserve consideration here and to which the reflections on intimacy developed in this article could also contribute.
5. At the end of the 1980s, the collapse of the Soviet Union prompted a terrible economic crisis in Cuba. From then onwards, the phenomenon of *jineterismo* acquired increased visibility, as more and more members of the Cuban population, especially among the younger generations, saw in informal engagements with tourists a way to satisfy their needs, desires, and aspirations. Scholars have pertinently emphasized how the designation of *jineterismo* remains largely contested and tends to operate along discriminatory lines of race, class, gender, and nation (Berg, 2004; Cabezas, 2009; Fernandez, 1999; Simoni, 2008a).
6. The 'Rasta' I got to know in tourism milieus in Havana were mainly Afro-Cuban men adopting a subculture style that may be summarily characterized as valorizing blackness and Afro-related cultural expressions, sporting dreadlocks and Rastafari-inspired accessories and clothing, and privileging a laid-back approach to tourists. These people generally self-identified, and were seen by others, as Rasta.
7. See for instance the articles in Cole and Thomas (1999), Hirsch and Wardlow (2006), and Padilla, Hirsch, Munoz-Laboy, Sember, and Parker (2007), as well as the writings of Povinelli (2006), Patico (2009), Faier (2007), and Hunter (2010).

References

Berg, M. L. (2004). Tourism and the revolutionary New Man: The specter of *Jineterismo* in late 'Special period' Cuba. *Focal – European Journal of Anthropology, 43*, 46–56.
Berger, P. L. (1973). 'Sincerity' and 'authenticity' in modern society. *Public Interest 31*, 81–90.

Brown, D. (1996). Genuine fakes. In T. Selwyn (Ed.), *The tourist image: Myths and myth making in tourism* (pp. 33–47). Chichester: John Wiley and Sons.

Bruner, E. M. (1994). Abraham Lincoln as authentic reproduction: A critique of postmodernism. *American Anthropologist, 96*(2), 397–415.

Cabezas, A. L. (2009). *Economies of desire: Sex and tourism in Cuba and the Dominican Republic.* Philadelphia, PA: Temple University Press.

Cohen, E. (1988). Authenticity and commoditisation in tourism. *Annals of Tourism Research, 15*(3), 371–386.

Cole, J., & Thomas, L. (Eds.). (2009). *Love in Africa.* Chicago: Chicago University Press.

Crick, M. (1992). Life in the informal sector: Streets guides in Kandy, Sri Lanka. In D. Harrison (Ed.), *Tourism and the less developed countries* (pp. 135–147). London/New York: Belhaven Press/ Halsted Press.

Crick, M. (1995). The anthropologist as tourist: An identity in question. In M.-F. Lanfant, J. B. Allcock, & E. M. Bruner (Eds.), *International tourism. Identity and change* (pp. 205–223). London: Sage.

Daniel, Y. P. (1996). Tourism dance performances: Authenticity and creativity. *Annals of Tourism Research, 23*(4), 780–797.

Enzensberger, H. M. (1996) [1958]. A theory of tourism. *New German Critique, 68,* 117–135.

Faier, L. (2007). Filipina migrants in rural Japan and their professions of love. *American Ethnologist, 34*(1), 148–162.

Fernandez, N. (1999). Back to the future? Women, race, and tourism in Cuba. In K. Kempadoo (Ed.), *Sun, sex, and gold: Tourism and sex work in the Caribbean* (pp. 81–89). Lanham: Rowman & Littlefield Publishers.

Frohlick, S. (2007). Fluid exchanges: The negotiation of intimacy between tourist women and local men in a transnational town in Caribbean Costa Rica. *City and Society, 19*(1), 139–168.

Goffman, E. (1959). *The presentation of self in everyday life.* Garden City: Doubleday.

Graburn, N. H. H. (1989). Tourism: The sacred journey. In V. L. Smith (Ed.) *Hosts and guests: the anthropology of tourism* (2nd ed., pp. 21–36). Philadelphia: University of Pennsylvania Press.

Graburn, N. H. H. (1983). The anthropology of tourism. *Annals of Tourism Research, 10*(1), 9–33.

Graburn, N. H. H. (2001). Secular ritual: A general theory of tourism. In V. L. Smith & M. Brent (Eds.), *Hosts and guests revisited: Tourism issues of the 21st century* (pp. 43–50). New York: Cognizant Communication Corporation.

Harrison, J. (2003). *Being a tourist: Finding meaning in pleasure travel.* Vancouver: University of British Columbia Press.

Hirsch, J. S., & Wardlow, H. (Eds.). (2006). *Modern loves: The anthropology of romantic love and companionate marriage.* Ann Arbor: University of Michigan Press.

Hom Cary, S. (2004). The tourist moment. *Annals of Tourism Research, 31*(1), 61–77.

Hunter, M. (2010). *Love in the time of AIDS: Inequality, gender and rights in South Africa.* Indianapolis: University of Indiana Press.

Kim, H., & Jamal, T. (2007). Touristic quest for existential authenticity. *Annals of Tourism Research, 34*(1), 281–301.

MacCannell, D. (1973). Staged authenticity: On arrangements of social space in tourist settings. *The American Journal of Sociology, 79*(3), 589–603.

MacCannell, D. (1976). *The tourist: A new theory of the leisure class.* London: Macmillan.

Mattingly, Ch. (2006). Pocahontas goes to the clinic: Popular culture as Lingua Franca in a cultural borderland. *American Anthropologist, 108*(3), 494–501.

McCabe, S. (2005). 'Who is a tourist?' A critical review. *Tourist Studies, 5*(1), 85–106.

Olsen, K. H. (2002). Authenticity as a concept in tourism research: The social organization of the experience of authenticity. *Tourist Studies, 2*(2), 159–182.

Padilla, M., Hirsch, J. S., Munoz-Laboy, M., Sember, R. E., & Parker, R. G. (Eds.). (2007). *Love and globalization: Transformations of intimacy in the contemporary world.* Nashville, TN: Vanderbilt University Press.

Palmié, S. (2004). *Fascinans* or *Tremendum?* Permutations of the state, the body, and the divine in late-twentieth-century Havana. *New West Indian Guide, 78*(3/4), 229–268.

Patico, J. (2009). For love, money, or normalcy: Meanings of strategy and sentiment in the Russian–American matchmaking industry. *Ethnos, 74*(3), 307–330.

Picard, D. (2011). *Tourism, magic and modernity: Cultivating the human garden.* Oxford: Berghahn.

Povinelli, E. A. (2006). *The empire of love: Tower a theory of intimacy, genealogy, and carnality.* Durham: Duke University Press.

Ryan, C. (1991). *Recreational tourism: A social science perspective*. London: Routledge.

Sant Cassia, P. (1999). Tradition, tourism and memory in Malta. *The Journal of the Royal Anthropological Institute, 5*(2), 247–263.

Selwyn, T. (1996). Introduction. In T. Selwyn (Ed.), *The tourist image: Myths and myth making in tourism* (pp. 1–32). Chichester: John Wiley and Sons.

Simoni, V. (2008a). Shifting power: The (de)stabilization of asymmetries in the realm of tourism in Cuba. *Tsansta: Review of the Swiss Anthropological Society, 13*, 89–97.

Simoni, V. (2008b). 'Riding' diversity: Cubans'/*Jineteros'* Uses of 'Nationality-talks' in the realm of their informal encounters with tourists. In P. Burns & M. Novelli (Eds.), *Tourism development: Growth, myths and inequalities* (pp. 68–84). Wallingford, CT: CAB International.

Simoni, V. (2012). Dancing tourists: Tourism, party and seduction in Cuba. In D. Picard & M. Robinson (Eds.), *Emotion in motion: Tourism, affect and transformation* (pp. 267–281). Farnham: Ashgate.

Simoni, V. (2013). Intimate stereotypes: The vicissitudes of being *Caliente* in touristic Cuba. *Civilisations: Revue internationale d'anthropologie et de sciences humaines, 62*(1–2), 181–197.

Simoni, V. (2014a). Revisiting hosts and guests: Ethnographic insights on touristic encounters from Cuba. *Journal of Tourism Challenges and Trends, 6*(2), 39–62.

Simoni, V. (2014b). Coping with ambiguous relationships: Sex, tourism and transformation in Cuba. *Journal of Tourism and Cultural Change, 12*(2), 166–183.

Simoni, V. (2014c). The morality of friendship in touristic Cuba. *Suomen Antropologi: Journal of the Finnish Anthropological Society, 39*(1), 19–36.

Simoni, V., & McCabe, S. (2008). From ethnographers to tourists and back again: On positioning issues in the anthropology of tourism. *Civilisations, 57*(1–2), 173–189.

Throop, J. C. (2014). Friendship as moral experience: Ethnographic dimensions and ethical reflections. *Suomen Antropologi: Journal of the Finnish Anthropological Society, 39*(1), 68–80.

Tucker, H. (2001). Tourists and troglodytes: Negotiating for sustainability. *Annals of Tourism Research, 28*(4), 868–891.

Wang, N. (1999). Rethinking authenticity in tourism experience. *Annals of Tourism Research, 26*, 349–370.

Zigon, J. (2013). On love: Remaking moral subjectivity in postrehabilitation Russia. *American Ethnologist, 40*(1), 201–215.

Index

Note: Page numbers in **bold** represent figures
      Page numbers followed by 'n' refer to notes

For Product Safety Concerns and Information please contact our EU representative GPSR@taylorandfrancis.com Taylor & Francis Verlag GmbH, Kaufingerstraße 24, 80331 München, Germany

Batch number: 08153807

Printed by Printforce, the Netherlands